SERIAL MURDER

Future Implications for Police Investigations

Robert D. Keppel

D1157186

anderson publishing co.
2035 reading road
cincinnati, ohio 45202
(513) 421-4142

SERIAL MURDER
Future Implications for Police Investigations

Copyright © 1989 by Anderson Publishing Co.

ISBN 0-932930-84-0
Libary of Congress Catalog Number 88-70142

Kelly Humble *Managing Editor*
Cover Design by Scott Burchett

Acknowledgments

I am grateful to several people for their help with this book.

The design of this book was conceptualized with the assistance of Charles Z. Smith, Professor Emeritus, University of Washington School of Law. His valuable suggestions and support led to the completion of this book in the format in which it currently exists.

Also, my thanks go to Stephen Michaud, Gregory Canova and Shirley Lindberg for their thoughtful editing of portions of this book.

Finally, special thanks go to those police investigators from all over the nation who have encourged me to write about this dynamic field of investigation.

CONTENTS

INTRODUCTION

Serial murder has become one of the central concerns in homicide investigation, both because of its apparent frequency and because of the unique problems it presents to investigative agencies. Above all, recent experience with serial killers has pointed out the inadequacies of the "reactive response" approach to investigating serial murder cases.

Traditionally, police and sheriff departments are organized to prevent burglaries and robberies, intervene in family fights, control traffic and provide other public services. They are not specifically organized to catch serial killers, who typically are not limited by jurisdictional boundaries. The investigation of serial murder is usually unprecedented, an extremely frustrating and difficult task for most police agencies. The investigation of the Yorkshire Ripper, Son of Sam, Theodore Bundy and the Hillside Strangler have demonstrated that existing police resources are inadequate, and routine investigative techniques are ineffective.

The most urgent calls for help in understanding the special problems of serial murder investigations have come from inexperienced police investigators, who, with mixed results, have turned for assistance to police consultants, forensic psychiatrists, clinical psychologists and criminologists in an often desperate search for special assistance. Additionally, the news media have made serial killer cases front page stories, creating even more confusion.

Sources of practical value to local law enforcement personnel faced with serial murder cases include the Violent Criminal Apprehension Program (VICAP), a nationwide clearinghouse for tracking serial killers, located at the FBI Academy, Quantico, Virginia. Also useful have been the handful of police consultants, experienced in serial murder investigation, who have advised on investigative management and apprehension strategies. Finally, many investigators have gained significant insights by attending periodic, multi-jurisdictional conferences where current cases and suspect information are discussed.

So far, however, one source of information about solving serial murders has remained virtually untapped. It is the case law on serial murder convictions.

Although the procedures used by police in homicide investigations have not been studied empirically, they are a common source of appellate issues raised by those convicted of murder and suspected of serial murder. Frequently, they illustrate that the successful completion of a serial homicide investigation is dependent on a combination of several so-called solvability factors. These are:

(1) The quality of police interviews with eyewitnesses.
(2) The circumstances which led to the initial stop of the murderer.
(3) The circumstances which established the probable cause to search and seize physical evidence from the person and/or the property of the murderer; specifically, the solvability factors in each case.
(4) The quality of the investigations at the crime scene(s)
(5) The quality of the scientific analysis of the physical evidence seized from the murderer and/or his property and its comparison to physical evidence recovered from the victims and the homicide scenes.

It is surprising that more empirical research has not been generated from the appellate cases which have criticized the quality of police investigations. Nor have detectives, traditionally, researched these investigative factors to make themselves more effective. To date, advances in the quality of detective work have been motivated and accomplished primarily by the ingenuity and drive of individual detectives.

Based on the cases of five notorious serial murderers, each of whom was convicted of at least one murder and suspected in at least twenty other murders, this text focuses on the major investigative and legal implications exhibited by these cases. The identified implications are applicable to serial murder cases in general.

This book's purpose is to identify those common investigative factors and trends that have been raised on appeal by convicted murderers in an effort to improve the investigative understanding of serial murder investigations. It is through these issues that implications for future serial murder investigations are derived.

The serial murderers chosen for this analysis are Larry Eyler, Wayne Williams, John Gacy, Theodore Bundy and Juan Corona. Each killer has already had an appeal argued before the highest state court. These appeals reflect directly upon the conduct of the police during the various stages of the investigation and, specifically, the solvability factors in each case.

Some convicted serial murderers, such as Gerald Stano, Kenneth Bianchi, Jerry Brutos, Richard Carpenter and many others, were considered and rejected for this analysis because their cases either (1) were not appealed because they pled guilty; (2) have not yet been argued before a state appellate court; or (3) have been appealed on other issues which did not affect the solvability factors in their investigations, e.g., the constitutionality of a state's death penalty statute.

A case study approach is presented in this text. Each of the referenced appellate cases includes a presentation of various aspects of the underlying police investigation. The cases include the citation to the appropriate source document:

(1) *People v. Eyler*, 87 Ill. Dec. 648, 132 Ill. App. 3d 792, 477 N.E.2d 774 (1985)

(2) *People v. Gacy*, 103 Ill.2d 1, 82 Ill. Dec. 391, 468 N.E.2d 1171 (1984)

(3) *Bundy v. State*, 455 So.2d 330 (Fla. 1984)

(4) *Williams v. State*, 251 Ga. 749, 312 S.E.2d 40 (1983)

(5) *People v. Corona*, 80 Cal. 3d 684, 145 Cal. Rptr. 894 (1978)

Appellate court decisions include a summary of the relevant testimony and other evidence presented at trial, the appellate court's analysis of the individual issues presented by the appeal, and the appellate court's decision. This text will follow that format, although in a condensed fashion. No other material, fiction or non-fiction, dealing with any of these convicted serial killers was used in preparing the five cases for this text. The court's conclusion and reasoning, issues on appeal and facts identified in the chapters of this text are excerpted and summarized from the appropriate court's opinion. In Chapter 1, the circumstances leading to the arrest and detention of Larry Eyler and the improper search of his truck are described. The issues for review presented by the state of Illinois are stated. The chapter closes with the appellate court's reasoning behind the affirmation of the county circuit court's judgments that the arrest and detention of Eyler were illegal.

Chapter 2 focuses on the facts leading to the identification of Wayne Williams as the Atlanta Child Murderer. Six issues brought on appeal by Williams are described and followed by the Georgia Supreme Court's reasoning to affirm Williams' conviction on two counts of murder.

In Chapter 3, the investigation into the disappearance of Robert Piest and subsequent excavation of the crawl space of John Gacy's home is presented. Gacy's issues on appeal are stated, and the chapter closes with the court's reasoning for affirming the thirty-three murder convictions of John Gacy.

Chapter 4 presents the facts surrounding the arrest of Juan Corona and the recovery of twenty-five bodies from gravesites located on ranches in Sutter County, California. Corona's only issue on appeal is identified and followed by the California Supreme Court's reasoning for granting a new trial to Corona.

The circumstances surrounding the investigation of Theodore Bundy for the Chi Omega sorority house murders and assaults are described in Chapter 5. Bundy's separate points on appeal are stated. The chapter closes with the Florida Supreme Court's reasoning for affirming the judgments of conviction.

Chapter 6 identifies the significant implications for police investigations in future serial murder cases; the final conclusions are stated in Chapter 7. An outline of procedures for investigators is also given. The chapter closes with the implications of legal issues raised on appeals which are followed by specific recommendations for investigators.

Based upon the experience of this author as an investigator and consultant in numerous high-profile serial murder cases, it is hoped that the reader will appreciate the importance of the stated implications. The text demonstrates that the analyses of the five cases add to a basic understanding of the serial murder investigation process. Any future analyses of other serial killers will greatly benefit law enforcement agencies that find themselves in the middle of a serial murder investigation.

Finally, the reader is cautioned to be aware of the limitations of any case study approach. The major problems are possible observer bias (the observer sees what he or she wants or is preconditioned to see) and attempts at generalization: "the insights which may be acquired concerning a particular case may not apply to any other case."[1]

Notes

[1] Gay, L.R. *Educational Research*. Charles E. Merrill Pub. Co., Columbus, Ohio 1976, p. 337.

CHAPTER 1

LARRY EYLER

The following facts, issues on appeal and appellate court's conclusion and reasoning are excerpted and summarized from the court's opinion in *People v. Eyler*, 87 Ill. Dec. 648, 132 Ill. App. 3d 792, 477 N.E.2d 774 (1985).

Facts

Prior to September 30, 1983, the states of Illinois and Indiana were experiencing the murders of young males. The bodies were discovered in remote areas. In each case the cause of death was stabbing. The victims were found partially dressed with their pants down.[1] A Central Indiana Multi-Agency Investigative Team (Task Force) was formed to review eight murder cases and to assist surrounding counties in murder investigations. It was also assisting in the investigation of three murders in Lake County, Illinois.[2]

Larry Eyler was named as a suspect in certain homosexual murders in a telephone tip received from an identified male who knew Eyler. He was also a suspect based upon other information gathered in investigating that call. However, there was no warrant for Eyler's arrest, and investigators lacked probable cause to arrest Eyler for the murders at that time.[3]

Further Task Force investigation of Larry Eyler revealed that in 1978 Eyler was arrested for stabbing a male he had tied up and disrobed while in a secluded, wooded area in Indiana. He was also involved in an incident in 1982, but not charged, when he picked up a male hitchhiker. The hitchhiker was given drugs and alcohol by Eyler and was subsequently abandoned in a secluded, wooded area of Indiana.[4]

While surveilling Eyler in July and August of 1983, the police observed him frequenting gay bars and picking up hitchhikers. He was observed picking up a hitchhiker in a section of Indianapolis where two of the murder victims had lived. Several murders in Illinois were linked by characteristics in the method of operation to the murders in Indiana. Eyler lived in Terre Haute, Indiana, but also went to Chicago, Illinois frequently.[5]

On September 30, 1983, at about 4 a.m., Indiana State Trooper Kenneth Buehrle was northbound on Interstate 65. He observed two men emerging from the southbound side of the Interstate. One of the men carried a bag. A silver pickup truck was parked on the shoulder of the road about fifteen yards south of the men. Parking along the Interstate was prohibited.[6]

Buehrle crossed the median and entered the southbound lanes. He stopped the silver pickup truck as it was driving away. The trooper questioned the driver, Larry Eyler, about his reason for stopping the vehicle. Buehrle asked for Eylers's drivers' license and vehicle registration. He also asked the passenger, Darl Hayward, for identification. When Buehrle asked what they were doing in the ditch, Eyler explained that he was going to the bathroom. Buehrle asked Hayward about the bag he was carrying. Hayward said it contained toilet paper. The trooper asked if he could look inside the bag. Buehrle observed that the bag contained personal items but no toilet paper. Hayward stated they had used all the paper.[7]

Eyler produced an Indiana driver's license and proper truck registration. Hayward also had identification. Buehrle asked Eyler to accompany him to the unmarked squad car in order to check his license. While Eyler sat on the passenger side of the squad car, Buehrle called on the radio for a warrant check. The trooper wrote a warning citation to Eyler for illegal parking on the Interstate. The dispatcher requested Buehrle's location in code which indicated to Buehrle that there was some sort of problem. However, Buehrle did not know what the trouble was.[8]

At the time Buehrle called the dispatcher, Sergeant Peter Popplewell was in the police radio room. The dispatcher told Popplewell that he believed Eyler was the suspect named on the police bulletin regarding certain murders. Larry Eyler had a similar name to "Larry Eyle" which was listed on the bulletin. The bulletin also indicated that "Larry Eyle" was named as only a possible suspect in some murders of a homosexual nature. The name "Eyler" was written "Eyle" on the original bulletin. Instructions were, however, that "Eyle" was not to be arrested.[9]

Popplewell then drove to Buehrle's location. Enroute, Popplewell received additional information about Eyler as a suspect in certain murders. Popplewell was instructed to bring Eyler and Hayward in for interrogation. The truck was to be impounded.[10]

Popplewell arrived at Buehrle's location and was joined by Sergeant Cothran. Eyler was removed from Buehrle's squad car. He was placed in the straddle position and patted down for weapons. Eyler was handcuffed and then locked in Buehrle's car with the seat belt secured around him. Hayward was still in Eyler's truck with the engine running. Hayward was then removed, patted down and handcuffed. Cothran checked the truck's interior for weapons when Hayward was removed.[11]

Buehrle told Cothran that the bag Hayward showed him was not the same bag he saw them carry from the ditch. Cothran then returned to the truck and searched the interior. Under the front seat Cothran located a second bag, lighter in color than the one Buehrle examined. The bag contained various lengths of rope and white tape. Cothran returned the bag to the truck.[12]

Sergeant Cothran drove Eyler to the police post. After arriving at the police post, Eyler's belt and boots were removed. He was placed in a holding cell. Hayward was in Popplewell's car awaiting a tow truck. Popplewell told Hayward that Eyler was a suspect in some homosexual killings. He also advised Hayward that he was a possible accomplice. Hayward then denied any knowledge of these homosexual killings.[13]

Hayward told Popplewell that he was hitchhiking from Chicago to Indianapolis when Eyler picked him up. While they drove from Illinois to Indiana, Eyler repeatedly offered $100 to Hayward for sexual purposes. Hayward said that he refused. He said that Eyler had made the offer while they were in Indiana.[14]

Hayward related that they had stopped along the Interstate because Eyler wanted to go to the bathroom. Eyler had repeated his offer near the ditch and displayed a $100 bill. Hayward said he again refused. Eyler had asked Hayward to pull up his shirt and Hayward had complied. Hayward related that Eyler said he "looked

great." Hayward admitted to Popplewell that he was homosexual.
Popplewell's interview of Hayward lasted twenty to twenty-five minutes.[15]

The Indiana State Police testified that Eyler was not under arrest. However, Eyler testified that he believed he was under arrest.
He also testified that he repeatedly asked the officers at the initial
stop what was happening, but was told nothing. At the police post
Eyler was informed that he was a suspect in a "major felony case."
Later, he was told he was being held for questioning with regard to
homosexual murders. When he asked if he would be allowed to
leave, Eyler was told that could be held for "pandering and prostitution."[16]

Issues on Appeal

The prosecution for the state of Illinois presented four issues
for review. They involved the initial determination by the trial court
that Eyler was illegally seized for the purposes of interrogation regarding certain murders. The issues were (1) whether probable
cause to arrest Eyler arose during a proper *Terry* stop (*Terry v. Ohio*,
392 U.S. 1, 88 S.Ct. 1868, 20 L.Ed.2d 889 (1968)); (2) whether probable cause to arrest Eyler for a separate crime arose based on the
statement of Hayward during the illegal seizure of the defendant;
(3) whether evidence found in Eyler's truck should not have been
suppressed because its discovery was inevitable; and (4) whether the
search warrant stated probable cause.[17]

Appellate Court's
Conclusion and Reasoning

The judgments of the Lake County Circuit Court were affirmed.
Larry Eyler was definitely not free to walk away from the officers.[18]
Whenever a person's freedom has been restrained in some way by a
police officer, a seizure has occurred.[19]

The fact that Eyler was immediately seized for purposes of interrogation regarding certain murders was not disputed. Searches of the ditch and truck were done after Eyler's seizure. The initial stop for a traffic violation was proper as well as Buerhle's request for a warrant check. However, there was no probable cause for Eyler's immediate interrogation detention. Eyler was named only as a *possible* suspect in the murders. The record shows no known criminal activity, other than the parking violation, at the time of his seizure.[20]

The facts demonstrate that Eyler had already been seized for purposes of questioning on several murders before a search of the area was conducted, and before Hayward made his statement about Eyler's prostitution violation.[21]

The court offered an alternative to the entire situation. The officers could have asked Eyler to come to the police precinct. A voluntary consent to accompany officers to a stationhouse for interrogation has been used by courts to distinguish between permissible stationhouse interrogation on less than probable cause from arrest due to illegal custodial interrogation.[22]

The actions of the police officers at the initial stop of Larry Eyler proved to be disastrous to his prosecution in several murder cases. It is not clear if the police bulletin was sufficiently ambiguous to confuse police officers about the disposition of Eyler after he was stopped. The bulletin indicated specifically that 'Eyle' was not to be arrested. Yet the court record did not indicate if the bulletin stated what officers should do, short of arrest, if 'Eyle' was stopped. No matter what the degree of ambiguity, the state troopers who initially confronted Eyler did not follow acceptable procedures for the search and detention of a possible suspect.

By contrast, in the next chapter a proper detention and search of Wayne Williams after his voluntary consent is addressed. Both the *Eyler* and *Williams* cases demonstrate that the initial stop of a murder suspect is a significant phase of a police investigation. It is also one that is highly scrutinized and frequently attacked on appeal by murder defendants.

Notes

[1] *People v. Eyler*, 87 Ill. Dec. 648, 132 Ill. App. 3d 792, 477 N.E.2d 774, 779 (1985).

[2] *Id*. at 778-779.

[3] *Id*. at 779.

[4] *Id*. at 781.

[5] *Id*.

[6] *Id*. at 777.

[7] *Id*.

[8] *Id*.

[9] *Id*. at 779.

[10] *Id*. at 777.

[11] *Id*.

[12] *Id*. at 777-778.

[13] *Id*. at 778.

[14] *Id*.

[15] *Id*.

[16] *Id*.

[17] *Id*. at 779.

[18] *Id*. at 781.

[19] *Id*. at 780.

[20] *Id*. at 781.

[21] *Id*. at 782.

[22] *Id*. at 784.

CHAPTER 2

WAYNE B. WILLIAMS

The following facts, issues on appeal and supreme court's conclusion and reasoning are excerpted and summarized from the court's opinion in *Williams v. State*, 251 Ga. 749, 312 S.E.2d 40 (Ga. 1983).

Facts

During the years 1979, 1980 and 1981, the city of Atlanta and some surrounding jurisdictions were experiencing the murders of more than seventeen adolescent and young adult black males. An Atlanta multi-agency police task force was established to investigate similar murders which were occurring in more than one jurisdiction.[1] As many as twenty-nine disappearances had occurred.[2]

Prior to May 22, 1981, the bodies of several young black males had been found in local rivers. The police speculated that these corpses had been thrown into the water from bridges, and the same might occur with other victims. Police strategically placed stakeout teams at several bridges over the Chattahoochee River. On the evening of May 22, a four-man surveillance team was stationed at the James Jackson Parkway Bridge.[3]

The stakeout teams consisted of FBI agent Gilliland and Atlanta Police Officer Holden, who were dressed in plain clothes and stationed at each end of the bridge in unmarked chase cars. Two Atlanta police recruits, Jacobs and Campbell, were positioned on foot on the west bank of the river. The location of team members permitted observation of headlight reflections from cars approaching from the west. In addition, cars entering the bridge from the west and traveling ten miles per hour or more passed over a metal expansion joint on the bridge.[4]

Early that morning a loud splash was heard. Officer Campbell thought the splash sounded like a human body hitting the water below the bridge. No lights had been observed up to that point, nor had the characteristic noise of the expansion joint been heard. The vehicular traffic was light at that hour, and a period of at least ten minutes elapsed between the time the last car was seen to cross the bridge and the sound of the splash. Shortly after the splash, a car's lights appeared on the bridge directly above where the splash had occurred. A white Chevrolet station wagon was observed unusually close to the edge of the bridge. It was traveling at about three to four milers per hour. The car was observed to exit the bridge and turn around in a nearby parking lot. It proceeded back across the bridge at about thirty-five to forty milers per hour. No other autos passed over the bridge during this incident.[5]

Subsequently, Wayne Williams was stopped by Gilliland and Holden while operating a white Chevrolet station wagon a short time later on Interstate 285. In the ensuing 90 minutes, Williams was interrogated and his vehicle searched with his consent. During the search, officers observed dog hairs, a nylon cord and a paper bag containing men's clothes. Williams gave officers false information while he was detained.[6]

On May 21, 1981, Nathaniel Cater, a 28 year-old black male, was last seen holding hands with Wayne Williams outside the Rialto Theater at about 9:15 p.m. Cater's body was discovered in the Chattahoochee River on May 24, 1981. Cater died by asphyxia due to some kind of chokehold. Cater's body was nude and several foreign fibers and hairs were recovered from his pubic and hair regions.[7]

On April 22, 1981, Jimmy Ray Payne was last seen standing by a taxi cab with Wayne Williams. A witness saw Williams and Payne talking to the taxi driver. A white station wagon was seen parked on the opposite side of the street, approximately one mile from the Chattahoochee River. Payne's body was discovered clad only in red shorts in the Chattahoochee River on April 27, 1981, a short distance from the location at which the Cater body was found.[8]

On June 3, 1981, Morris Redding, Chief of the Atlanta Task Force, appeared before a superior court judge to request a warrant authorizing a search of William's car and residence. The following facts and circumstances were Redding's affidavit: (1) a description of seventeen Task Force victims, the cause of their deaths, and the fact that the state crime lab analysis had revealed the presence of microscopic fibers or dog hairs, or both, on each of the bodies; (2) the circumstances of the May 22 Jackson Parkway Bridge stop of Williams, including the search of his car and observations of dog hairs, a nylon cord and a paper bag containing men's clothes; (3) the subsequent police investigation leading to the alleged discovery that Williams gave false information to officers who questioned him on May 22; (4) and the details of police surveillance of Williams which was conducted subsequent to the May 22 stop. A search warrant was issued.[9]

On June 22, Redding applied for a second warrant with an affidavit which was identical to the earlier affidavit, except that 123 new paragraphs describing the June 3 search were appended to the initial 157 paragraphs. The additional paragraphs stated that certain fibers recovered in that search were determined by scientific tests to be "microscopically identical" to fibers found on the bodies of sixteen of the Task Force victims. Redding requested that another search be allowed in order to gather evidence to corroborate the results of scientific tests already performed. The warrant was issued.[10]

In reviewing Williams' conviction for two murders, the Supreme Court of Georgia offered comparative profiles of each of the homicides, charged and uncharged (see Appendix). These profiles illustrate the similarities of the victims and their deaths (modus operandi), the logical connections of all of the homicides and the evidence that Williams was the perpetrator of each.[11]

Issues on Appeal

Even though Wayne Williams brought over thirty enumerations of error on appeal, only six are considered for the purposes of the report.

Williams' enumerations of error included (1) that the state failed to adequately demonstrate the scientific reliability of the fiber methodology which was employed by its experts;[12] (2) that he was denied his due process right to have experts of his choosing examine fiber evidence possessed by the state crime laboratory;[13] (3) that the evidence of ten homicides which were not the subject of this trial was admitted;[14] (4) that Lee Brown, Commissioner of Public Safety, improperly testified as to the organization and responsibilities of a police task force;[15] (5) that his right to suppress statements he gave to police and observations they made in the course of his detention on May 22 should have been upheld;[16] and (6) that, regardless of the legality of the initial Interstate 285 stop and any consent he may have subsequently given, his prolonged detention by police exceeded the scope of a *Terry*-type stop (*Terry v. Ohio*, 392 U.S. 1, 88 S.Ct. 1868, 20 L.Ed.2d 889 (1968)) and became a full-fledged arrest which was not supported by probable cause, and was thus illegal.[17]

Supreme Court's Conclusion and Reasoning

The Supreme Court of Georgia examined Williams's assignments of error and found them to be without merit. Judgment was affirmed.

(1) The state's experts testified that they believed certain of the fibers which were associated with the twelve victims matched others that had been recovered from Williams' home and cars. It was their opinion that these matches established an inference that Williams had been in contact with the victims before their deaths. This opinion was relied on by the prosecutor to support the further inference that Williams had killed the victims.[18]

It is for the trial court to determine whether a given scientific principle or technique is competent evidence. The trial court bases its determination upon evidence presented to it at trial by the parties (i.e., testimony, exhibits, treatises and the rationale of cases in other jurisdictions).[19]

(2) Williams did not have an absolute, unqualified right to examine the fiber evidence. The motion for an independent examination must be timely and include the critical evidence a defendant seeks to inspect. If the defendant knows, or in the exercise of reasonable diligence should know, of the existence of potentially critical evidence in the possession of the state, yet fails to move in a timely

fashion for its examination, then he cannot claim unfair surprise by its introduction at trial.[20]

Despite the fact that the trial began December 28, it was not until February 1 that Williams apprised the court that he was dissatisfied with the court's harmless omission to authorize his expert to inspect that evidence. On at least two occasions (January 18 and February 17) defense experts were in fact offered the opportunity to look at fibers in question, but declined to so.[21]

(3) The purposes for which evidence of ten other homicides (extrinsic offenses) may be offered include identity, motive, intent, absence of mistake or accident (each is an aspect of intent) and a plan or scheme that is part of the crime. To render evidence of extrinsic offenses admissible for any of these purposes, the state must show that the defendant was the perpetrator of the extrinsic offenses. Moreover, there must be a sufficient similarity or connection between the extrinsic offense and the offense charged, so that proof of the former tends to prove the latter.[22]

A determination of this issue depends on an analysis of the facts surrounding the two charged murders and the ten uncharged homicides. Part of the evidence used by the state to connect Williams with these homicides consisted of the comparison of fibers and hairs discovered on the victim's clothing, bodies and/or items used in recovery of their bodies, with fibers and hairs removed from Williams, his home and cars and his German Shepherd dog.[23]

Each of the homicide victims was a young black male from a low-income home in the metropolitan Atlanta area whose lifestyle placed him alone on the streets. They had communality of appearance and behavior. Each was connected to Williams by animal hair and fibers. Many of the victims were actually seen by third parties in the company of Williams, although Williams continually maintained that he did not know and had not associated with any of the victims. Eight of the ten males suffered death by asphyxiation. The other two, one stabbed and one bludgeoned, were linked by other characteristics. Twelve homicides with these common characteristics shows a definite pattern.[24]

Additionally, the Court considered testimony given by witnesses who had conversations with Williams. Williams had a negative attitude toward black children from lower class backgrounds. Williams expressed anger and shame when discussing "street kids" and would make derogatory comments about his own race. Williams told an acquaintance that he had compiled statistical data on the reduction of the black male population by the elimination of one black male. Another young black male, who had seen the victim Geter with Williams, related that he had been approached by Williams about a job and got into Williams' car and rode around with him. Williams fondled him, and when Williams stopped the car to get something out of the trunk he ran away. The above facts support the Court's stated profile information.[25]

(4) Lee Brown, Atlanta's Public Safety Commissioner, testified about the organization and responsibilities of the police task force. Brown testified that task forces are usually organized because they are a proven vehicle for conducting investigation into similar murders which occur in more than one jurisdiction. He said that a task force was organized in Atlanta to investigate a pattern of crimes involving the deaths of young black children. He also testified that in April 1981 the task force staked out bridges over rivers in the metropolitan Atlanta area in an attempt to apprehend whoever was responsible for throwing bodies into rivers. Williams objected to the reference to these other crimes and to the use of the word pattern.[26]

The Court found that Brown did not state the number of pattern deaths to which he referred, and, as they had already determined, evidence of ten independent or "pattern" crimes was properly admitted over a period of several days at trial.[27]

(5) The initial stop of Williams was justified under *Terry v. Ohio*, and Williams's consent to the ensuing detention and search of his automobile was given voluntarily and was not the result of duress or coercion. A valid consent eliminates the need for either probable cause to search or a search warrant.[28]

The Court's review of the record concluded that Williams was never formally arrested on May 22. The officers at the scene of the bridge had probable cause under *Terry v. Ohio* to detain Williams and question him thoroughly concerning his presence on the Jackson Parkway Bridge. The facts and circumstances known by the officers, including the recent dumping of the body of Jimmy Ray

Payne in the area, the silent and unseen approach of Williams's car to the bridge and the loud splash heard by Campbell at the same time the car appeared to have been stopped on the bridge, warranted, in a person of reasonable caution, the belief that a crime had been committed by Williams. The rationale satisfies *Terry v. Ohio* in that investigating officers who possess articulable suspicion of criminal activity can detain a suspect for a limited period in order to identify the suspect, frisk him if necessary and conduct limited questioning.[29]

Williams's reasoning that his prolonged detention became a full-fledged arrest was not accepted by the Court. The critical factor was that Williams' own testimony established that he consented to being questioned and having his car searched.[30]

In *Williams v. State*, the Georgia Supreme Court revealed its willingness to permit testimony about related offenses. Thorough investigation into the circumstances surrounding a victim's disappearance in similar cases is necessary. Even though there may be insufficient evidence to file murder charges in these extrinsic offenses, they may provide crucial evidence to prove common scheme and connection to the case in question.

The *Williams* cases in Atlanta represented a special circumstance when a task force was formed to investigate a series of missing and murdered children. In the next chapter, the John Gacy investigation features a traditional, but thorough, investigation of a missing juvenile that uncovered the homicides of more than thirty victims. Thus the formation of a task force came about to investigate and identify found bodies after the identity of the murderer was known.

Most importantly, the *Gacy* cases will address how detailed law enforcement officers must be in describing the circumstances surrounding the disappearance of a missing person in an affidavit for a search warrant.

Notes

[1] *Williams v. State*, 251 Ga. 749, 312 S.E.2d 40, 72 (1983).

[2] Brown, Lee P. Department of Public Safety, City of Atlanta, "Background Material Missing and Murdered Children's Cases." 1981.

[3] *Williams v. State*, 251 Ga. 749, 312 S.E.2d 40, 75 (Ga. 1983).

[4] *Id*. at 75.

[5] *Id*.

[6] *Id*. at 77.

[7] *Id*. at 54-55.

[8] *Id*. at 54.

[9] *Id*. at 77.

[10] Id. at 77-78.

[11] *Id*. at 63.

[12] *Id*. at 48.

[13] *Id*.

[14] *Id*. at 51.

[15] *Id*. at 72.

[16] *Id*. at 75.

[17] *Id*. at 76.

[18] *Id*. at 48.

[19] *Id*.

[20] *Id*. at 49.

[21] *Id*.

[22] *Id*. at 51.

[23] *Id*. at 52.

[24] *Id*. at 70-71.

[25] *Id*. at 71.

[26] *Id*. at 72.

[27] *Id*.

[28] *Id*. at 76.

[29] *Id*. at 77.

[30] *Id*. at 76.

CHAPTER 3

JOHN GACY

The following facts, issues on appeal and supreme court's conclusion and reasoning are excerpted and summarized from the court's opinion in *People v. Gacy*, 103 Ill.2d 1, 82 Ill. Dec. 391, 468 N.E.2d 1171 (1984).

Facts

On December 11, 1978, Robert Piest, a fifteen-year-old white male, was working at the Nisson Pharmacy in Des Plaines, Illinois. He worked with fellow employee Kim Byers. Byers told police that Piest asked her to "come watch the register; that contractor guy wants to talk with me. I'll be right back." Piest went outside of the store to meet with John Wayne Gacy. Piest's mother was also in the store at this time and was waiting to take her son home from work. Prior to leaving the store her son requested that she wait a few minutes while he spoke to the contractor about a summer construction job. Mrs. Piest waited over twenty minutes in the store and then began looking for her son. Robert Piest left the store at about 9:00 p.m. and never returned. Mrs. Piest immediately reported her son missing to the Des Plaines Police Department.[1]

John Gacy was observed in the store on December 11 on two occasions: at 6 p.m. and at 8:00 p.m. He remained in the store until 8:50 p.m. Police verified that Gacy was, in fact, a contractor and owned PDM Construction Company in Norridge, Illinois, a suburb of Chicago. The police learned that Gacy had a record for sexually assaulting young men and had been convicted in Iowa for an assault on a teenage boy.[2]

On December 13 a search warrant was granted to search Gacy's residence and vehicles for the clothing of Robert Piest, along with hair samples, blood-stained clothing and dried blood samples.[3] Police confiscated fifty-seven items, including a receipt for film left to be developed at Nisson's Drug Store and a Maine West High School

31

class ring. It was learned that the receipt was in Piest's possession when he disappeared and the class ring was owned by John Szyc, who had previously been reported missing. The police photographed a television set in Gacy's home, and it appeared to be similar to one which had been taken from Szyc's apartment.[4]

On December 21, 1978 an additional search warrant was authorized to search Gacy's home for the body of Robert Piest. This warrant was based upon additional facts noted below. Subsequent investigation revealed that the film receipt was in the possession of Robert Piest immediately prior to the time he disappeared.[5]

The affidavit also stated that Officer Robert Schulz, who had been surveilling Gacy, had informed the affiant, Lieutenant Kozenczak, that he had been invited into Gacy's home by Gacy while on the surveillance unit assigned to watch Gacy. While inside, Schulz said he detected "an odor similar to that of a putrefied human body."[6]

Excavation of the crawl space of Gacy's home and the area surrounding his home recovered twenty-nine bodies. In the course of the investigation Gacy admitted to police that he had killed approximately thirty individuals, some buried in the crawl space under his home and five thrown into the Des Plaines River. Four bodies were ultimately recovered from the Des Plaines and Illinois rivers, downstream from the place where Gacy told police he had thrown the bodies.[7]

John Gacy was convicted on thirty-three counts of murder.

Issues on Appeal

Gacy raised over fifty issues on appeal. Only four issues are considered for this report. Gacy claimed that (1) the initial search warrant failed to satisfy the "basis of knowledge" test of *Aguilar v. Texas*, 378 U.S. 108, 84 S. Ct. 1509, 12 L. Ed.2d 723 (1964) and failed to disclose sufficient facts to establish probable cause;[8] (2) the application for the search warrant was factually defective in that it failed to state the time when the informants made their observations;[9] (3) the search warrant failed to describe with particularity the items to be seized, and the warrant caused the scope of the search to be too broad and constituted an impermissible general search;[10] and (4) his first confession was not the product of a rational mind or free will.[11]

Supreme Court's Conclusion and Reasoning

The judgments of thirty-three convictions were affirmed.

(1) In considering Gacy's first issue on appeal, the Supreme Court of Illinois was guided by *Spinelli v. U.S.*, 393 U.S. 410, 89 S.Ct. 584, 21 L.Ed.2d 637 (1969). In that case the U.S. Supreme Court ruled "that only the probability, and not a prima facie showing, of criminal activity is the standard for probable cause."[12] Gacy claimed that the affiant's statements were conclusional and did not identify the sources of his information. That the complaint does not set forth in detail how one of the witnesses was able to identify John Gacy as the contractor with whom Piest went to speak is not a fatal defect. Furthermore, much of the hearsay information was received from the victim's mother and not from an undisclosed professional informant.[13]

In addition, the Court did not agree with Gacy that it was not indicative that a crime had been committed but only "unusual" or "suspicious" when a fifteen-year-old boy stated that he was going to speak with the suspect, left his place of employment and then failed to return. The assertion that the affidavit for search warrant contained insufficient facts to establish probable cause is without merit.[14]

(2) By not stating the time when informants made their observations, Gacy claims this made the affidavit defective. Gacy points out that the affidavit only stated that Lieutenant Kozenczak had received this information on December 11, 1978, but does not indicate on what date Piest was last seen at the drugstore. Gacy suggests that "missing person cases may remain unsolved for weeks, months, or years." Gacy concluded that "without more specific information regarding time, a reasonable person could not have concluded that

evidence of the alleged offenses was presently on the premises to be searched." The Court disagreed. A common sense reading of the affidavit indicates that Lieutenant Kozenczak received this information while investigating a missing person report at Nisson Pharmacy on December 11, 1978.[15]

(3) Gacy argued that "because there was no indication as to the alleged owner of the clothing or items to be seized, no mention of any sizes, styles or manufacturers, and no explanation as to why the items might be evidence of a crime, the warrant authorized a general search. Gacy also pointed out that the inventory of items seized listed fifty-seven objects, only one of which, a blue jacket, was listed in the warrant. Naturally, two items, a receipt for film left to be developed at Nisson's Drug Store and a Maine West High School class ring, were particularly significant and not listed on the warrant.[16]

Concerning the Maine West High School ring, the police were aware that Piest lived in Des Plaines, was fifteen years old and that there was a high probability that Piest attended this high school. Although the ring did not bear Piest's initials, the police officer conducting the search may not have immediately noticed the initials on the ring, and, in any event, the police were aware that Gacy could very well be a habitual sex offender and that more than one victim could be involved. The film receipt which was found in Gacy's wastebasket showed that film had been left for development at Nisson's Pharmacy. The Court found no error in seizing the receipt or ring.[17]

(4) Two days before Gacy's arrest, he asked a police officer to inform his attorney in the event of his arrest. Gacy claimed that the police officer's failure to communicate with Gacy's attorney before questioning him violated his rights. Gacy also contended that his first confession was not the product of a rational mind.[18]

Gacy's supposed invocation of his right to counsel when talking to Officer Hackmeister was apparently no more than a request that the officer contact Gacy's attorney when he was finally arrested, because Gacy had received money from out of state to be used to post his bond. The record shows that Gacy was in continuous contact with his attorneys during the days prior to his arrest and that on the night before his arrest he had told his attorneys that he was responsible for thirty-three murders. Gacy was read his rights and signed a waiver form given him by the Des Plaines Police Department.[19]

Nothing in the record supports Gacy's contention that his confessions were not the product of a free and a rational mind. The failure to assert his objection at trial precluded the circuit court from making a record on this point so that the Supreme Court could properly review such a contention.[20]

The facts in this appeal demonstrate the importance of a thorough follow-up investigation of a missing person report. This comprehensive investigation into the disappearance of Robert Piest led to the discovery of over thirty additional murders. In the following chapter, a suspicious circumstances investigation is presented which led to the discovery of the twenty-five victims of Juan Corona. The Gacy and Corona cases exemplify how a seemingly routine case can expand into a complex serial murder investigation.

Notes

[1] *People v. Gacy*, 82 Ill. Dec. 391, 103 Ill.2d 1, 468 N.E.2d 1171, 1176-1177 (1984).

[2] *Id*. at 1177.

[3] *Id*.

[4] *Id*. at 1179.

[5] *Id*. at 1180.

[6] *Id*.

[7] *Id*. at 1176.

[8] *Id*. at 1177.

[9] *Id*. at 1178.

[10] Id. at 1174.

[11] *Id*. at 1180-1181.

[12] *Id*. at 1177.

[13] *Id.* at 1178.

[14] *Id.*

[15] *Id.* at 1178-1179.

[16] *Id.* at 1179.

[17] *Id.*

[18] *Id.* at 1181.

[19] *Id.*

[20] *Id.*

CHAPTER 4

JUAN CORONA

Juan Vallejo Corona was found guilty of twenty-five counts of First Degree Murder. The following facts, issues on appeal and supreme court's conclusion and reasoning are excerpted and summarized from the court's opinion in *People v. Corona*, 80 Cal. 3d 684, 145 Cal. Rptr. 894 (1978).

Facts

On May 19, 1971 at about 10:00 a.m., Mr. Kagehiro found a hole in the northeast corner of his peach orchard. The hole was about 7' long, 3 1/2' to 4' deep, and 30" wide. The dirt had been piled up alongside the hole. At about 6:00 p.m., Kagehiro returned to the hole; the dirt had been filled back in. Kagehiro called the police. The following morning the police uncovered the filled-in hole and found the body of Kenneth Whitacre. The victim was lying on his back with his right arm extended over his head and left arm across his chest. His shirt was pulled over his head. Whitacre had suffered a blow to the back of the head caused by a machete or machete-like instrument. Also, there was a stab wound in his chest. Whitacre had been dead less than twenty-four hours.[1]

Eyewitnesses placed Whitacre in the general area of the Kagehiro farm at about 1:00 p.m. on May 19. Between 8:00 and 8:30 p.m., David and Sharon Schmidt saw a red and white pickup truck near the crime scene. The pickup bore the inscription "Juan V. Corona, Labor Contractor" on the side. There was no one in the pickup. While Sharon Schmidt was waiting for her husband, who had walked over to the river, she saw Corona come out of the brush, get into his vehicle and leave in a hurry. Police recovered tire impressions from the scene that were made by the same kind of tires that were on Corona's van.[2]

Since the discovery of the Whitacre murder showed common hallmarks of all the subsequent recovered bodies as well, the proof surrounding Whitacre's death and Corona's connection with it gains special significance.[3]

Corona's connection with the killings became more apparent when a third gravesite was discovered. The body of victim number three, Melford Sample, suffered the same type of wounds as Whitacre's: hacking in the back of the head and stab wounds in the left chest. More importantly, about six to eight inches above Sample's feet two pieces of pink paper were found. They were slips from the Del Pero Meat Company, dated May 21, 1971, and bore the name of Juan Corona. One piece of paper was signed by Juan Corona, who had purchased meat from the Del Pero meatcutter. Corona's signature indicated a charge for the meat as he did not pay cash for it. Corona had folded the two slips together while at Del Pero's and placed them in his right shirt pocket.[4]

A police search recovered twenty-five bodies from gravesites located on the Sullivan and Kagehiro ranches in the Marysville/Yuba City area of Sutter County, California between May 20 and June 4, 1971.[5]

With the exception of Whitacre, the exact dates of deaths of the victims could not be determined. Evidence strongly indicated that the pattern of the killings and the *modus operandi* employed by Corona were strikingly similar.[6]

Twenty-four of the twenty-five victims had received one or more chop-type or hacking-type injuries to the head. The chop wounds were of two kinds: 'slashing wounds probably inflicted with a light weapon, such as a knife, and severe chop wounds caused by a heavy instrument such as a bolo machete. The latter wounds typically appeared in a horizontal direction covering the face, head and ear, and were inflicted with a force of such magnitude that they cut the bone and severed the lower parts of the skull. The other common pattern was the infliction of stab wounds in the upper left chest of the victims by using a cutting instrument which penetrated the heart or lung and severed the aorta leading from the heart to the lungs.[7]

The common *modus operandi* was further bolstered by the circumstances that the victims were buried in the same general area in a manner which was likewise similar, if not identical. Almost without exception, each of the victims was lying on his back with his hands over his head, chest or stomach, and his shirt or other clothes pulled over the head. In at least seven graves the underwear of the victims was pulled off or removed, exposing the penis and genital area, giving rise to the inference that the crimes may have been sexually motivated, and that the perpetrator may have been a homosexual.[8]

Corona was connected to the crimes by an intricate and elaborate set of circumstantial evidence. To begin with, at all relevant times Corona was employed as a labor contractor for the Kagehiro and Sullivan ranches. He hired and supervised itinerant farmworkers who did seasonal harvesting and thinning jobs in the orchards. He had unquestionable access to the area of the gravesites and was seen by several eyewitnesses in the area of the homicides at crucial times.[9]

In the twenty-fifth grave, the burial ground of Joseph Maczak, the police discovered a number of items (candleholder, pieces of broken mirror, child's sock). More importantly, two Bank of America deposit slips were found in Maczak's grave. Printed on the slips was "Juan V. Corona, 768 Richland Road, Yuba City, California."[10]

On May 26 Corona was arrested and search warrants were served. Corona's office facility yielded the following evidence: a glass candleholder described as red, green and yellow glass, Spanish writing on it which resembled the broken glass candleholder located in Maczak's grave. In Corona's mess hall desk a 9 mm Browning pistol was found. Bullets from this pistol matched bullets found in the head of the eleventh victim, William Kemp. In the drawer with the gun was a long knife that appeared to have coagulated blood on it near the sheath. On the blade the words "Tennessee Toothpick" were inscribed. Hanging on a nail in the kitchen were several receipts from Del Pero Brothers market made out to Juan Corona and signed at the bottom, "Juan Corona." Another item discovered in the mess hall was a pen that wrote in five different colors. The ink from this pen matched the colors of ink in a green ledger found in Corona's bedroom.[11] This so-called "death ledger" has seven of the victims names written in it.

Other items seized from Corona's car and house include: a post hole digger covered with dried mud with hairs imbedded in the mud, throw rugs with blood stains on them, boots with blood on them and a blood-stained van.[12]

The ensuing laboratory examination of the items seized in the search of the mess hall, the Corona house and garage revealed human blood from all four universal blood groups.[13]

On May 3 or 5, 1971, Byron Shannon, labor contractor, met John Henry Jackson, victim twenty-one, who was looking for a job. Before they could make any arrangements, Corona came by in his pickup and hired Jackson. This was the last time anyone saw Jackson alive. A similar occurrence took place on May 12, 1971. On that occasion Shannon was talking to Smallwood, Allen, and Riley (Victims 15, 16 and 17). Corona drove up, and they accepted a job offer from him. Shannon never saw any of three men again. Other similar sightings of victims in contact with Corona were observed by witnesses.[14]

Corona's neighbor, Beatrice Valdez, observed Corona on numerous occasions drive past between 6:45 and 7:00 p.m. and return within two to two-and-one-half hours. Corona did not always use the same vehicle; sometimes he drove his impala, sometimes his van and sometimes his pickup. On returning, he usually washed his vehicle. He would never really wash them completely but would just hose out the inside.[15]

The following background facts were additionally described by the Court:

> Corona was represented at the trial by Richard E. Hawk, a privately retained sole practitioner. Since Corona was not able to pay the substantial amount of attorney's fees chargeable in a case of such magnitude, a fee agreement was entered into between the parties. Pursuant to the agreement, Hawk was granted exclusive literary and dramatic property rights to Corona's life story, including the

proceedings against him, in return for legal services. Under the agreement, Corona expressly waived the attorney-client privilege, thereby removing any impediment to the publication of the most intimate and confidential details of his life and his trial. The surrender of all-inclusive publication rights and the attorney-client privilege was irrevocable and in perpetuity binding not only on Corona, but also his heirs, executors, legal representatives and assigns. The income derived from the publications was to inure solely and exclusively to Hawk. In the wake of the agreement, Hawk hired Ed Cray, a professional writer who participated in the proceedings as Hawk's investigator and sat at the counsel table during the trial. Well before the commencement of the trial, Cray and Hawk entered into a contract with the MacMillan Publishing Company to publish the book to be written about Corona and his trial. The book, entitled *Burden of Proof, The Case of Juan Corona*, authored by Cray and supplemented by Hawk's afterword, was published just a few months after the completion of the trial.[16]

After about five days of deliberation, the jury brought in its verdict finding Corona guilty of First Degree Murder on all twenty-five counts charged.[17]

Issues on Appeal

Corona assailed his conviction on a number of grounds, but the central contention advanced on appeal was that Corona was deprived of effective assistance of counsel.[18] Even though this contention does not relate directly to any individual solvability factor, the California Supreme Court's conclusions and reasoning to grant Corona a new trial do directly express how Corona's defense counsel should have properly attacked the prosecution's witnesses and evidence.

Supreme Court's
Conclusion and Reasoning

The judgment of the trial court was reversed.

Despite the wide ranging and elaborately woven web of circumstantial evidence connecting Corona to the crime and unerringly pointing to his participation in their commission, trial counsel for Corona failed to raise the obvious alternative defenses of mental incompetence and/or diminished capacity and/or legal insanity. Still worse, Corona's lawyer failed to present any meaningful defense at all. After a lengthy trial lasting several months, in which the prosecution produced more than one hundred lay and expert witnesses and put in an immense wealth of documentary evidence, Corona's lawyer failed to call a single witness on his client's behalf, and submitted the case basically upon the evidence produced by the prosecution.[19]

The California Supreme Court summed up the necessity of a possible insanity defense by stating:

> [A]pellant's mental competence, capacity, and legal sanity were called into question by (1) the very nature of the crimes, i.e., the senselessness and savagery of the murders committed without any apparent motivation; (2) the mental history of Corona, showing the existence fo schizophrenia, paranoia and psychosis as far back a 1956; (3) the result of current psychiatric examinations conducted by several psychiatrists in 1971-1972, which confirmed one way or another the recurrence of Corona's old mental illness; (4) the high dosage of Thorazine administered to the patient, which by itself was indicative of the seriousness of the current psychosis; and finally (5) the almost unanimous recommendation of psychiatrists that Corona be placed in a mental institution for further observation, examination and treatment.[20]

The insanity issues aside, Corona's lawyer failed to develop any of the defenses he promised in his opening statement. The alibi defenses relate specifically to the solvability factors developed by police. They were: (1) that the proof of Corona's whereabouts was in question on the crucial date of May 19, 1971, when Whitacre, the first victim discovered, was murdered; (2) that Corona had a leg infection and was not able to walk during the crucial period from the end of March to the middle of April 1971; (3) that others also had access to the knives with which the killings were done; (4) that the blood in Corona's van originated from an injured person who was taken by Corona to a doctor; (5) that the killings were homosexual murders and Corona was heterosexual, having a balanced, happy marriage; and (6) that character witnesses, including a priest, would testify that Corona was a peaceful, religious man and a good father incapable of violence.[21]

The court was confronted with the unprecedented situation where Corona's lawyer assumed a position virtually adverse to his client and, totally unsupported by strategic or tactical consideration, took deliberate steps to thwart the development of viable defenses available to Corona.[22]

The court's decision on the Corona cases emphasized that police investigative procedures should have been the sources of an adequate defense by Corona's lawyer. In the next chapter, Theodore Bundy's appeal specifically attacked the methods that the police used to investigate the Chi Omega murders and a related assault.

Notes

[1] *People v. Corona*, 80 Cal. 3d 684, 145 Cal. Rptr. 894, 898 (1978).

[2] *Id.* at 899.

[3] *Id.* at 898.

[4] *Id.* at 899.

[5] *Id.*

[6] *Id.* at 898.

[7] *Id.*

[8] *Id.*

[9] *Id.*

[10] Id. at 899.

[11] *Id.* at 899-900.

[12] *Id.* at 900.

[13] *Id.*

[14] *Id.* at 901-902.

[15] *Id.* at 902.

[16] *Id.* at 903-904.

[17] *Id.* at 903.

[18] *Id.*

[19] *Id.*

[20] *Id.* at 907-908.

[21] *Id.* at 914.

[22] *Id.* at 916.

CHAPTER 5

THEODORE BUNDY

Theodore Bundy was found guilty of two counts of First Degree Murder, three counts of Attempted First Degree Murder and two counts of Burglary.[1] The following facts, issues on appeal, and the supreme court's conclusion and reasoning are excerpted and summarized from the court's opinion in *Bundy v. State*, 455 So.2d 330 (Fla. 1984). [Sidebar: Bundy has also been convicted and given the death penalty for the murder of Kimberly Leach in Lake City, Florida. At the time of his arrest for the Leach and Chi Omega murders, Bundy was wanted for escape and homicide in Colorado and was a suspect in 36 sex-related murders in the northwest United States.[2]]

Facts

On January 7, 1978, Bundy rented a room, under an assumed name, at The Oak, a rooming house near the Florida State University campus. During the evening hours of Saturday, January 14, Bundy was seen in a barroom next door to the Chi Omega sorority house. Two women testified that they were in the bar that night and subsequently identified Bundy as having been there.[3]

At approximately 3:00 a.m. on Sunday, January 15, 1978, Nita Neary arrived at the Chi Omega house from a date. She entered through a back door. She walked toward the front entrance hall, where the main stairway was located. At the same time, Neary heard the sounds of someone running down the stairs. When she arrived at the front entrance hall, she saw a man holding a club in his right hand, with his left hand on the doorknob. He was in the process of leaving the house. Nita Neary saw a right-side profile of the man's face. She saw him for several seconds before he left.[4]

Ms. Neary then went upstairs to her room, awakened her roommate and told her a description of the intruder and what she had seen. At trial, her roommate testified that Neary told her that the man wore light-colored pants, a dark jacket and skiing cap. The man had a protruding nose and carried a large stick with cloth tied around it. While Ms. Neary, her roommate, and another house resident discussed whether to report the incident to the police, Karen Chandler, a beating victim, emerged from her room. They could see that Chandler had been injured so they summoned medical help and the police. The severity of the intruder's actions was soon discovered: Lisa Levy and Margaret Bowman had been killed; Karen Chandler and Kathy Kleiner had been assaulted while asleep and could not describe their attacker.[5]

The cause of death for Lisa Levy and Margaret Bowman was strangulation. Additionally, they received severe beatings from what was discovered to be a length of a tree branch used as a club. Margaret Bowman's skull was crushed and laid open. Lisa Levy had been bitten with sufficient intensity to leave indentations which could clearly be identified as human bite marks. As a part of the investigation, police technicians took numerous photographs of the bite on the victim's body.[6]

While at the Chi Omega House, one officer obtained a description of the intruder from Nita Neary. The officer later testified that Neary told him the intruder was a young white male, cleanshaven, with a dark complexion, about five feet, eight inches tall, weighing about 160 pounds, wearing a dark toboggan cap, a dark waist-length jacket, light-colored pants and carrying a large stick.[7]

At the same time police officers were taking statements and processing the homicide scene, another attack was taking place only a few blocks away from the Chi Omega House. At about 4:00 a.m. on Sunday, January 15, two residents of a duplex apartment on Dunwoody Street heard loud noises coming from their adjacent apartment. They telephoned Cheryl Thomas, their next-door neighbor, and received no answer. They then called the police. After the police arrived and entered Thomas' apartment, officers discovered that Thomas was lying in her bed and severely beaten. Since she was attacked while sleeping, she could not describe or identify her attacker. Police investigators found in Thomas' room a knotted pair of pantyhose, which did not belong to Thomas. The pantyhose had holes which would indicate they were used as a mask.[8]

Two men who knew Bundy arrived at The Oak rooming house at about 5:00 a.m. on Sunday, January 15, 1978. One of the men lived there. As they proceeded inside to a room, they saw Bundy standing in front of the house looking in the direction of campus and the scenes of the crimes. As they passed him, both men casually greeted Bundy, but he did not acknowledge.[9]

At about noon on Sunday, several residents of The Oak and Bundy discussed the news of the crimes. One resident testified that during this conversation he speculated that the perpetrator was "some lunatic" who was "now probably hiding out real scared." Bundy disagreed by explaining that the crimes were "a professional job;" the killer was someone who had committed such crimes before and had probably already departed the area.[10]

On Sunday, January 15, Nita Neary met with investigators and again described the intruder. An artist made sketches of the intruder based on Ms. Neary's description. These sketches were admitted into evidence at trial. One week later, Ms. Neary was placed under hypnosis and again questioned concerning what she had seen in the foyer of the sorority house. During the hypnosis session, Ms. Neary added that she had seen brown hair hanging out of the man's ski cap and had also seen the man's eyebrows. These references were the only factual elements obtained through hypnosis that had not already been learned form Ms. Neary's previous descriptions. While testifying at trial, she stated that after the hypnosis session she did not remember seeing the brown hair or eyebrows on the night of the crimes.[11]

On February 11, 1978 at about 1:45 a.m., a Tallahassee police officer saw Bundy standing beside a car parked in the same campus neighborhood where both the crime scenes and The Oak rooming house are located. The officer confronted Bundy and asked him what he was doing there. While interviewing Bundy, the officer saw an unexpired automobile license plate inside the car and asked to see it. Bundy gave the tag number to the officer. As the officer walked to his car to call in the suspicious number, Bundy ran away, and the officer was unable to pursue him.[12]

Theodore Bundy was arrested in Pensacola, Florida on February 15, 1978 at about 1:30 a.m. A Pensacola police officer stopped Bundy and attempted to arrest him for car theft. The reason for the arrest and charge was kept from the jury at the trial. The officer tried to handcuff Bundy, but he struck the officer and fled. The officer fired a shot at Bundy. He pursued, overtook and subdued Bundy. On the way to jail, Bundy stated he wished the officer had killed him and then asked, "If I run at jail, will you shoot me then?"[13]

In April 1978 Bundy was in custody. This time, a detective from the Leon County Sheriff's Department in Pensacola traveled to Muncie, Indiana to conduct a photographic identification array procedure with Nita Neary. Previously, the investigator had cautioned Ms. Neary to avoid looking at news media photographs and reports to the effect that Bundy was a principal suspect. Neary selected Bundy's photograph from the montage. Neary later testified at trial that the man who she had seen was a white male in his twenties, about five feet, eight inches tall, weighing about 165 pounds, and with a prominent, straight-bridged nose that almost came to a point. Additionally, the intruder was clean shaven, had thin lips and was slightly dark in complexion. She had seen a right-side profile of his face. He wore a dark blue ski cap pulled down to his eyebrows and over his ear, a dark waist-length jacket and light colored pants. At trial, Nita Neary pointed out Bundy as the man she saw in the sorority house.[14]

A criminalist testified at trial that she removed several human hairs from the knotted pantyhose found in Cheryl Thomas's room. These hairs were subjected to microscopic examination and were compared to the head hairs taken from Bundy. The analyst concluded that the human hairs found on the pantyhose had the same characteristics as Bundy's and could have come from Bundy.[15]

Pursuant to a judge's warrant, law enforcement authorities arranged for a forensic dentist to obtain wax impressions and photographs of Bundy's teeth. The original photographs of the bite marks were enlarged to actual size. The models of Bundy's dentition were cast from the wax impressions. The forensic dentist testified that he looked at the particular features of Bundy's teeth and compared them to the indentations in Lisa Levy's flesh as revealed in the photographs. The dentist described his technique and analysis in detail. All materials were exhibited to the jury. The expert expressed to the jury his opinion that the indentations on Levy's body were left by the teeth of Bundy. Using computer-enhanced photographs of the bite marks, another expert came to the same conclusion. The second expert explained his theory of comparison. Both experts agreed that because of the wide variation in the characteristics of human dentition, individuals are so highly unique that the technique of bite mark comparison can provide identification with a high degree of reliability.[16]

Issues on Appeal

Theodore Bundy raised over twenty separate issues on appeal. For purposes of this report, four issues relate specifically to the solvability factors in his cases.

Bundy's separate points on appeal were (1) that the eyewitness identification of Nita Neary should have been excluded because prior to trial she was hypnotized for the purpose of improving the quality and detail of her recollection of the man she saw leaving the sorority house;[17] (2) that his right to due process of law was violated because an impermissibly suggestive photographic selection procedure was used which affected Ms. Neary's testimony to Bundy's prejudice;[18] (3) that the trial court erred in denying his motion to sever counts six and seven, which pertained to the crimes that occurred at the Cheryl Thomas apartment, from the remaining counts;[19] and (4) that the trial court erred in permitting the state to present testimony of dental experts who analyzed the bite inflicted on murder victim Lisa Levy and compared it to models of Bundy's teeth.[20]

Supreme Court's Conclusion and Reasoning

The judgments of conviction and sentences of death were affirmed.

(1) The Florida Supreme Court found that, based upon Ms. Neary's testimony, the hypnotic session did not add to or change her essential description of the man she saw.[21]

The court stated:

> From the time of her initial statements on the morning of the crimes, through all her interviews by police, through all her pretrial statements, up to and including her in-court description of the man she saw, Ms. Neary's description remained substantially consistent.[22]

The court further stated:

> This is not a case where the state relied at trial on the technique of hypnosis to show how an improved recall of past events was obtained. It is not a case where the state sought to present an expert to state an opinion as to the accuracy or reliability of testimony derived from a hypnotic examination. It is not a case where the state sought to refer to the technique of hypnosis to bolster the credibility of a previously hypnotized witness. The matter of the hypnosis was only raised by the defendant's motion to suppress Nita Neary's testimony.

> ...Under these circumstances, we do not hesitate to hold that the fact that hypnosis took place was a matter relating only to the weight of the testimony and not to its admissibility. Furthermore, under these circumstances the burden was on the defense to establish that the hypnosis rendered the testimony so unreliable as to be inadmissible and this it failed to do.[23]

(2) Bundy claimed that Ms. Neary had seen a photograph in the newspaper which may have influenced her choice from a police array of photographs. The court related that in some previous cases an impermissibly suggestive photographic identification does not apply to situations where a witness had earlier observed a picture of a defendant in the news media. Others have found that there was not a substantial likelihood of misidentification where, as in this case, the witness asserted that seeing the suspect's picture in the news media did not influence his or her identification. Ms. Neary testified that the newspaper photographs had no effect on her because they were not profiles. Her view of the intruder was a profile and so was the picture she selected from the lineup. Because Bundy failed to show that the police used an impermissibly suggestive procedure in obtaining an identification, the court found the Ms. Neary's identification testimony was properly admitted.[24]

Additionally, Bundy claimed that the police made a suggestive comment when an officer asked her to "select the photograph of the person that resembled the suspect." The court stated, "This remark implying that the suspect's picture was included in the array of '10' photographs did not render the procedure impermissibly suggestive."[25]

(3) On the issue of severing counts six and seven the court stated:

Two or more offenses are properly joined if they are based "on two or more connected acts or transactions."[26]

Additionally, the court considered the temporal and geographical association, the nature of the crimes and the manner in which they were committed.

Here the crimes occurred within a few blocks of each other and within the space of a couple of hours. The crimes were similar in that they involved a person entering the residences of female students in an off-campus neighborhood and beating young white women with a club as they slept. Hence the criminal acts are connected by the close proximity in time and location, by their nature, and by the manner in which they were perpetrated.[27]

(4) Bundy moved to exclude dental testimony on the ground that the comparison techniques were not reliable. The court explained:

> Bite mark comparison evidence differs from many other kinds of scientific evidence such as blood tests, "breathalyzer" tests, and radar (as well as from inadmissible techniques such as the polygraph and voice-print analyses) in that these various techniques involve total reliance on scientific interpretation to establish a question of fact. With bite marks evidence, on the other hand, the jury is able to see the comparison for itself by looking directly at the physical evidence in the form of photographs and models.[28]

The probative value of bite mark comparison in a case is for the trier of fact to determine. Bundy offered no basis for finding that the trial judge abused his discretion in allowing the bite mark evidence to be admitted.[29]

The Theodore Bundy appeal and the previous four cases presented in this text demonstrate not only an appellate court's willingness to review but also give careful consideration to the police methods used in investigation. From these cases, one can identify the answers to questions in how to handle the process involved in the investigation of future serial murder cases.

These cases point to the following serious questions that law enforcement agencies must be prepared to deal with in the future. Under what circumstances have the police broken from tradition and chosen to form a task force to investigate these difficult cases? How can a killer continue to murder without discovery? What is the importance of the living witness or victim? How do serial killers get caught? What interviewing techniques are most important in serial murder cases? On what occasions are arrest, search and seizure attacked on appeal? The answers to these questions, in addition to issues such as mobile killers, murders of opportunity, crime scene investigation and police conduct, are dealt with in the next two chapters.

Notes

[1] *Bundy v. State*, 455 So.2d 330 (Fla. 1984).

[2] *Bundy v. State*, 455 So.2d 9 (1985).

[3] *Bundy v. State*, 455 So.2d 330 (Fla. 1984) at 334.

[4] *Id.* at 334-335.

[5] *Id.* at 335.

[6] *Id.*

[7] *Id.*

[8] *Id.*

[9] *Id.*

[10] *Id.*

[11] Id. at 335-336.

[12] *Id.* at 336.

[13] *Id.*

[14] *Id.* at 336.

[15] *Id.*

[16] *Id.* at 337.

[17] *Id.* at 337.

[18] *Id.* at 343.

[19] *Id.* at 344.

[20] *Id*. at 348.

[21] *Id*. at 342.

[22] *Id*.

[23] *Id*.

[24] *Id*. at 343.

[25] *Id*.

[26] *Id*. at 345.

[27] *Id*.

[28] *Id*. at 349.

[29] *Id*.

CHAPTER 6

IMPLICATIONS FOR POLICE INVESTIGATIONS

Task Force Organization

The five preceding case studies reveal two different types of investigations that have confronted law enforcement agencies: (1) those jurisdictions that formed a task force to review continuing murder cases and to coordinate multiple investigations when the perpetrator was not known (Williams, Bundy and Eyler); and (2) those jurisdictions that organized a task force after the murderer was identified and many bodies discovered in a central location (Gacy and Corona). This forming of a task force for serial murder investigation is, for the most part, wholly unprecedented for the involved departments and considered a very non-traditional approach to homicide investigation.

When a department investigates an unsolved murder series with traditional policies and procedures, it can soon find itself faced with tremendous volumes of incoming information that will confound investigative cohesiveness. Without exception, unsolved serial murder investigations are characterized by difficulties in each of these areas: numerous victims, hundreds or thousands of suspects, hundreds of acquaintances of victims, little or no physical evidence directly leading to a suspect, cross-jurisdictional offenses, thousands of telephone contacts, "pride of authorship" problems between individual detectives and administrators within one department, lack of experienced personnel to investigate and supervise the cases, inadequate experience in establishing a priority system for lead follow-up, improper press relations and ill-conceived filing procedures for case information. All these problems result in many unfollowed leads left to be investigated and create an atmosphere of always being several steps behind in the investigation.

The establishment of a task force by several police agencies has been one method to deal effectively with these problems. Lee Brown, Atlanta's Public Safety Commissioner, testified in the Wayne Williams trial that task forces are usually organized because they are a proven vehicle for conducting investigations into similar murders which occur in more than one jurisdiction.[1] An additional problem unique to the creation of a task force is that homicide investigation by this method is usually a new and untried experience for the affected departments. If safeguards are not taken to assure proper lines of communication, provide adequate commitment of resources and personnel, establish mutual goals and assure proper investigative priorities, the task force can be fraught with the hidden agendas of individual departments and difficulties in dealing with the parochial attitudes of its members.

Murders of Opportunity

An unfortunate implication in analyzing the cases of these particular convicted murderers is that all were well into their series and had committed many murders before they were initially arrested. The following is a recapitulation for each convicted murderer of the number of murder convictions and the number of murders they were suspected of committing.

Name	Murder Convictions	Suspected Murders
Larry Eyler[2]	1	20
Wayne Williams[3]	2	28
John Gacy[4]	33	33
Juan Corona[5]	25	25
Ted Bundy[6]	3	36

Each murderer was able to kill over long periods of time, in some cases over a year or more, without any apparent threat of apprehension. In Bundy's case, he had escaped from a Colorado jail pending a First Degree Murder charge and was subsequently arrested in Florida for three murders that he apparently committed while on escape status.

These multiple murderers had the unique ability to control their impulses and restrict their homicidal behavior to those occasions when there was the least possible chance of detection. Initially, the convicted murderers were opportunists and did not want to get caught. Based upon the number of times they were sighted in their respective victim contact areas, the murderers were in constant search of potential victims. At the time these sightings were not considered unusual activity for the particular areas. These killers were as much a part of their surroundings as anyone else and were not doing anything which would unduly draw attention to themselves.

In most cases the convicted murderers were, at initial approach to their potential victims, unalarming and charismatic. The victims were doing various activities which included (1) sleeping in their bedrooms in multiple person dwellings, (2) looking for a job, (3) meeting people in a tavern, (4) soliciting for prostitution, (5) being approached while walking on a college campus and (6) hitchhiking. These opportunistic activities were easily exploited by these serial killers.

A significant interview technique regarding the normal activities of victims and suspects is recommended for situations where the police question potential witnesses while canvassing victim contact areas as well as body recovery sites. Police commonly ask people if they observed anything unusual or out of place. A more appropriate line of questioning is, perhaps, what the witnesses saw that was usual and normal for that particular area. Very rarely will the serial killer be seen running down the middle of a road with a bloody knife in his hand. With the exception of Bundy's sighting in the Chi Omega house, these serial killers operated for a long period of time without any actual witnesses to any one murder. Most of the witnesses observed these murderers in victim contact areas, apparently doing nothing out of the ordinary and not drawing attention to themselves.

Living Witnesses

Bundy, Gacy, Eyler and Williams had living victims or witnesses who testified against them. For reasons known only to the killer, the circumstances were inopportune for these witnesses to become homicide victims. The presence of living victims in these cases remains a favorable implication for future investigations. These individuals may provide the necessary facts of similar offenses to strengthen search warrant affidavits and the probable cause for arrest. The pursuit of these witnesses by investigators must be thorough and unending.

Some living victims and witnesses surfaced in these investigations prior to the identity of the suspect becoming known. Other witnesses were discovered after the murderer's name and description were published by the news media. In either situation, police investigators must exercise care in interviewing and handling potential witnesses.

The entire interview process with any witness or living victim is highly scrutinized by defense attorneys. Such testimonies are frequently used as issues on appeal. Bundy attacked the police conduct in the interview of Nita Neary on three separate issues. As a review from Chapter 5, these attacks were for an improper photographic identification after Bundy's photograph had appeared in the newspaper; the fact that Neary was hypnotized, and the suggestive comment of the officer who displayed the montage to Neary.

The actual documentation of each interview can be extremely important, as noted in the Bundy appeal. Nita Neary was interviewed several times by the police and had given several pretrial statements. The court noted that Neary's statements did not appreciably change from her initial statement to her final testimony. The documentation of each interview was valuable in proving the credibility of Neary's recollection from one statement to another.

Mobile Killers

The excessive number of victims these killers pursued (in addition to the number of separate occasions they were spotted in victim contact areas) indicate that these murderers used their ability to be mobile as a part of their continued method of operation. This common profile reveals that serial killers are highly mobile, frequently cruising and drawn to those victim contact areas where they feel they are in their 'comfort zone.' This significant behavior leaves the killers vulnerable to common police proactive measures, which consist of periodic and covert surveillances of quality suspects and areas. Surveillance may increase the likelihood of developing first-hand information for search warrant affidavits and probable cause to arrest. Surveillance was used for these purposes in the *Eyler*, *Williams* and *Gacy* cases.

Each of these killers had no shortage of vehicles available to them. Wayne Williams had as many as five different automobiles, which included the white station wagon that he was driving on the day he was stopped. Juan Corona had a van, a pickup truck and an Impala sedan. His neighbor observed Corona return each night and wash out the inside of each vehicle. John Gacy utilized his sedan and trucks registered to his construction company. Larry Eyler used his silver pickup for his travels between Indiana and Illinois. Theodore Bundy had available to him whatever vehicle he could steal.

Most of the killers were observed by witnesses in a moving vehicle or near a vehicle they were ultimately seen driving. Some were either stopped or observed driving on freeways. Eyler was stopped by the Indiana State Police for a freeway parking violation. Williams was finally stopped on a freeway after being followed from the bridge incident.

These killers became very familiar with the victim contact areas as well as the body recovery areas. This general observation is based upon the continued frequency with which they picked up victims in similar geographic areas. Additionally, Bundy, Williams, Gacy and Corona had body dump sites where more than one victim was recovered. Gacy used the crawl space under his residence, and

Corona buried bodies on property to which he had immediate access. Bundy and Williams would leave a victim from one time period in a remote area and return to the same location to deposit another victim.

The discovery of a multiple body recovery site where victims have been deposited at different times should alert authorities that they are probably faced with a serial murder investigation. Determining the pattern of related murder cases can be a difficult process, especially if the victims are found alone, in a skeletal condition and in separate jurisdictions. However, in the case of a multiple body recovery site, the determination of a serial homicide should be obvious.

In any event, police authorities would be wise to assume the widest connotation in considering the method of operation factors in related murders. A strict adherence to perfect traditional "M.O." factors may carelessly eliminate a related murder. In the Wayne Williams cases, two murder victims had different causes of death than the other ten related victims. Other characteristics and evidence connected to Williams linked these cases to the pattern.

Apprehension

Author Donald Lunde, in *Murder and Madness*, notes that if sadistic killers are not caught, they are likely to repeat their murders.[8] A popular belief has been voiced in the news media that serial killers are caught by "luck." This belief is somewhat reinforced by the book *Killing One Another*, when author Gwynn Nettler states, "These hate-filled men are sometimes caught after their first murder, usually by luck."[7] However, Nettler did not expand on the term "luck" to define its relationship to any solvability factor.

The reality of the five murderers presented here is that they were arrested through normal, routine police procedures. The police in each case narrowed their investigation when the identity of the potential suspect was discovered. Larry Eyler was identified after he had been stopped by the Indiana State Police for a routine parking violation along a freeway. A name similar to Eyler was known to the police task force investigating the pattern of murders. The traffic stop precipitated the investigation and directed the focus upon Eyler.

Wayne Williams was first arrested after a strategic surveillance of bridges was initiated by the Atlanta Task Force investigating the similar murders of black children. The pattern of dumping bodies into local rivers at bridge locations was identified, and a creative surveillance network was established. The stop of Williams after a splash was heard by an officer, and the subsequent careful and thorough police investigation, led to his arrest and successful prosecution for murder.

John Gacy was contacted by police after his name came up in a routine missing person investigation. A patient and thorough follow-up investigation was accomplished in the disappearance of Gacy's last known victim. Gacy's ultimate arrest was consummated after Gacy voluntarily invited a surveillance officer into his house. The officer then smelled what was known to him as decaying human remains. This fact and other probable cause elements resulted in a comprehensive search warrant affidavit. The ensuing search of Gacy's home and Gacy's confession led to the discovery of thirty-three murder victims.

The investigation which led to the arrest of Juan Corona followed a different track. A property owner discovered a freshly dug hole about the size of a grave. The next day, he returned to find that the hole had been filled with dirt. He reported this to police who disinterred the last victim of Juan Corona. Subsequent investigation revealed the bodies of twenty-four more victims as well as a wide-ranging and elaborately woven web of circumstantial evidence connecting Corona to the murders.

Theodore Bundy was stopped and arrested by a police officer in Pensacola, Florida for operating a stolen vehicle. A police task force investigating the deaths of two girls at the Chi Omega sorority in Tallahassee was notified. Subsequent investigation placing Bundy in the Tallahassee area at the time of the murders and linking Bundy to physical and circumstantial evidence at the Chi Omega sorority and surrounding area led to his arrest and conviction in those murders.

In each case, a major police follow-up investigation was prompted by duties that officers routinely perform every day. To the credit of the follow-up officers, quiet, subtle leads were converted into successful investigations. This fact alone should alert police investigators to the potential source of solving a serial murder.

Monitoring local and neighboring police patrol activities should be a priority in the investigation of serial murders. This requires extremely well conceived and properly monitored communications among investigative units and patrol officers. Periodic briefings should occur by attending roll calls and conferences, or through producing informative video tapes. The briefings encourage information sharing, as well as serve to update patrol officers on what information has been developed and what information is needed. In the case of Larry Eyler, a breakdown in communication resulted in police officers misinterpreting a bulletin sent out by task force investigators. Police officers held Eyler for questioning in various murders without proper authority.

Much has been said about the serial murderer actually catching himself, but what usually occurs is that some patrol officer, on routine duty, comes across the killer. It then takes alert and intelligent investigators to turn this opportunity into a final resolution of the case. In many serial murder investigations, the investigators have the name of the killer early in the investigation, and the patrol contact triggers renewed interest in the particular suspect.

Physical Evidence Considerations

Despite the news media portrayal of serial killers as clever, intelligent, media conscious, conniving and careful, the fact remains that they really do not cover their tracks very well. In every instance, these serial killers were apprehended in possession of trace evidence or implements of their crimes. Their homes and vehicles contained hairs, fibers, bloodstains and other evidence that connected them to various victims.

It is obvious from the number of exhibits admitted into evidence at trial that the police collected and logged hundreds of items of evidence associated with each serial killer. This fact necessitates the establishment of complete and accurate police procedure outlining the collection of evidence. A proper chain of custody for each piece must be maintained. Police agencies could be faced at any time with crime scene processing of the magnitude in the Gacy and Corona properties. A prescribed and well conceived standing operating procedure is essential for evidence collection, the logging of evidence items and cross-referencing each item as it relates in importance to other items logged.

Destruction or loss of evidence is always a major concern, especially if it can be proven that destruction was unfavorable to the accused. Loss of evidence due to poor tracking and record maintenance is inexcusable. Not only will evidence be processed by local and federal crime laboratories, but every piece of evidence should be inspected by defense experts. Proper handling and accountability for each piece of evidence is vital.

Tight controls must be kept on publication of recovered physical evidence that is crucial to the police investigation. During the Wayne Williams investigation, "in February 1981, an Atlanta newspaper article publicized that several different fiber types had been found on two murder victims. Following publication of this article, bodies recovered from rivers in the Atlanta metropolitan area were found either nude or clothed only in undershorts. It appeared possible that the victims were being disposed of in this undressed state and in rivers in order to eliminate fibers from being discovered on their bodies."[9]

Interviewing Considerations

Experience in these serial murder cases has demonstrated that a high investigative priority must be given to isolating, as accurately as possible, the dates and times victims were last seen and to delineating their activity patterns up to their disappearance. The dates, times and facts surrounding victim disappearances were extensively stated in the various search warrant affidavits. Furthermore, accurate dates and times can be useful in comparing a suspect's whereabouts with the last known activity of any victim.

Any information received from witnesses about dates, times and facts surrounding a disappearance must be thoroughly corroborated. Further questioning of witnesses as to why they believe they saw the victim on a certain date and at a particular time is important. Proper interrogation of suspects requires focusing on these times and dates as accurately as possible.

As these serial murder investigations progressed, the number of victims and witnesses increased. It is vital to assure that all witnesses and potential suspects are asked all the proper questions. An interviewing strategy plan for all witnesses in serial murder cases is recommended. With numerous investigators questioning many witnesses and potential suspects, it is important that all investigators interview from the same frame of reference.

Notes

[1] *State v. Williams*, at 72.

[2] *Chicago Tribune*, August 23, 1984.

[3] Brown, Lee P. 1981.

[4] *People v. Gacy*, 103 Ill.2d 1, 82 Ill Dec. 391, 468 N.E.2d 1171 (Ill. 1984).

[5] *People v. Corona*, 80 Cal. 3 d 684, 145 Cal. Rptr. 894 (1978).

[6] *Bundy v. State*, 471 So. 2d 9 (1985).

[7] Nettler, Gwynn. *Killing One Another* (Cincinnati: Anderson Publ. Co., 1982) p. 135.

[8] Lunde, Donald T. *Murder and Madness* (N.Y.: W. W. Norton Co., 1979) p. 53.

[9] Deadman, Harold A. "Fiber Evidence and the Wayne Williams Trial," *FBI Law Enforcement Bulletin*, May 1984, p. 10.

CHAPTER 7

CONCLUSION

Part I: Outline of Procedure for Investigators

The following conclusion outlines recommended procedures for police investigators involved in the investigation of serial murder. It reflects a step-by-step approach from initial report to conclusion at trial.

Investigative Technique

Initial Report. Whether the initial report is originally a missing person case or the discovery of unidentified remains, a complete and thorough investigation into the identification of the victim and the circumstances surrounding the disappearance is vital. It is from this information that the basis for further inquiry is established.

At the earliest possible time, investigators must determine if the disappearance or homicide investigation is related to others in a series. Naturally, the discovery of a multiple body recovery site where the victims have been deposited at different times indicates a serial murder case.

The most effective method of dealing with the investigative problems in serial murder cases is through the formation of a team of detectives or task force. A unified effort causes investigators to deal with all aspects of the investigation in a coordinated manner.

In considering the method of operation (M.O.) factors in related murders, police investigators must assume the widest connotation. When considered collectively, partial suspect information in separate, but similar, cases may hold the key solvability factors for the entire serial murder case.

Interviewing Techniques. As already discussed, the highest investigative priority must be given to isolating the dates and times victims were last seen and to delineating their activity patterns up to their disappearance. This information must be thoroughly corroborated because facts and circumstances may change throughout the duration of the investigation. Witnesses who are recontacted at a later date may forget important details. The longer the investigation progresses, the more distant in time circumstances become. Proper interrogation of suspects requires focusing on these times and dates.

All interviews must be conducted from the same frame of reference. This requires that all investigators be familiar with a strategic interviewing plan that is developed for the particular serial murder investigation at hand. The facts of any one investigation dictate the elements of the plan. The plan must include the proper questions to ask all persons interviewed.

Due to the frequency with which a suspect visits the victim contact areas, a thorough and exhaustive canvass for witnesses or living victims must be completed. In past serial murder cases, these individuals have provided the necessary facts from similar offenses that strengthened search warrant affidavits.

The actual documentation of any interview, oral or written, is vital to the final resolution of the case. This documentation protects the credibility of witnesses and exemplifies the thoroughness of the police investigation.

Crime Scene Investigation. The investigation of the crime scene includes, but is not limited to, the documentation, photography, diagraming and collection of all pertinent physical evidence. The crime scene not only includes the body recovery site but also the murder sites, victim contact area and the suspect's body, residence and vehicles. High quality crime scene processing is required in each of these areas. No less emphasis in processing should take place just because a found body is determined to be a body dump location. In prior serial murder cases, hairs, fibers, bloodstains and other trace evidence were found in these important areas that were connected to suspects and victims.

An additional consideration at crime scenes is the tight control of information about discovered physical evidence. A press release policy must be established to protect the information crucial to the investigation, and these guidelines must be strictly followed by all investigators.

Scientific Analysis of Physical Evidence. The earliest involvement of crime laboratory personnel is recommended. Their presence at the crime scene assists in determining evidence collection procedures for certain types of evidence that they will be required to examine and compare. Additionally, crime lab personnel are familiar with current procedures for evidence collection and logging of evidence items. The familiarity with this procedure enables the crime lab to cross-reference each item as it relates in comparison and importance to other items. Proper handling and accountability for each piece of evidence is vital to the continuity of the case.

Search and Seizure. Evidence can come into the hands of the police at any stage of the investigation. In prior serial murder cases, a police officer on routine patrol has frequently confronted the suspect. Periodic briefings of patrol officers on the important aspects of the investigation must be accomplished so there are no miscommunications between investigators and patrol officers in seizing evidence at the initial stop of the suspect.

Investigators must keep a continuing search warrant affidavit containing all pertinent facts as the investigation progresses. This procedure enables investigators to reduce time-consuming affidavit preparations at the time of arrest. If this procedure is followed, many investigators examining volumes of files simultaneously will not be necessary.

Advice on Constitutional Rights. At the point of custodial interrogation, advice of rights is required. The advice of rights is not enough, but a clear waiver of rights is equally required before custodial statements are admissible. In prior serial murder cases, suspects gave alibi and confession statements.

Investigation of Suspects. Serial murder cases involve the investigation of many potential suspects. The establishment of a priority system for past and incoming suspects and their elimination is essential. The lack of a clear priority system results in some suspects being partially investigated, their elimination postponed by investigations of a "better" suspect, resulting in a situation of catch-up and the feeling of being overwhelmed by masses of work.

There is a danger in using elimination criteria unless it is conclusive. The wrong suspect could be eliminated. The alibi for any suspect on the dates and times considered important to the investigation must be immediately checked and corroborated.

Preparation for Trial

All police reports and original officer notes must be complete and ready to undergo the scrutiny of defense attorneys. Additionally, all evidence must be cataloged, cross-referenced and the chain of custody maintained. The evidence will be analyzed by defense experts. The condition of the evidence must be unquestionable.

Current addresses and telephone numbers for all witnesses must be kept updated. During long investigations, witnesses frequently move and their whereabouts may be in doubt.

Testimony at Trial

During the testimony of the defendant, an experienced FBI criminal profiler should be present to assist the prosecutor in determining questions for cross-examination. This assistance enables the prosecutor to reveal a different personality than that presented to the jury on direct examination.

In serial murder cases, hundreds of exhibits are entered at trial by prosecutors through police testimony. If any one investigator is involved in lengthy testimony, the investigator must be prepared and not appear monotonous in this verbal testimony. Also the investigator must be able to readily identify each exhibit that is to be introduced through his testimony.

The testimony at trial of all police officers, witnesses and crime laboratory personnel is a reflection of the overall case preparation

and investigation. Serial murder cases are characteristically compli-
cated to investigate. All the follow-up activities of police investigators are highly scrutinized by defense attorneys. These case require
consultation with prosecuting attorneys. Constant and active coor-
dination when legal issues arise during the course of the investigation will reduce problems at pretrial hearings and trial.

Part II: Legal Issues Raised on Appeal

The legal issues raised on appeal in the *Eyler, Gacy, Bundy,
Williams* and *Corona* cases attacked the police conduct in interviewing witnesses, the initial confrontation of the suspect by police
and the search of the suspect's property. Even though each of these
defendants had many issues on appeal, these three general issues directly effected the police investigation and were addressed by the
appellate courts in those cases. Each of these three areas are summarized specifically as they relate to each defendant's case and the
legal concepts involved. These recommendations are for law enforcement officers involved in a serial murder case and can aid in
more efficient investigation and more effective and constitutional
prosecution.

Police Conduct in Interviewing Witnesses

Bundy and Eyler attacked the police interview techniques for
different reasons. Bundy's points on appeal were (1) that the eyewitness' identification to the Chi Omega murders should have been
excluded because the witness was hypnotized, and (2) that his right
to due process was violated because an impermissibly suggestive
photographic selection procedure was used to identify him.

Usually the burden is on the defense to establish that hypnosis
renders testimony unreliable. In this particular case, the witness's
accounts of what she saw did not vary from her initial statements after hypnosis. Fortunately, the police recorded detailed reports each

time the witness was interviewed. This procedure contributed to providing the credibility of the witness's statements.

As pointed out by the Supreme Court of Florida, case law varies from one state to another. Testimony after hypnosis is admitted in some states if it can be shown that the hypnosis interview was not suggestive and/or that the testimony was not different from previous statements. In other states, any testimony after hypnosis is inadmissible. This requirement does not preclude the police from using hypnosis as an investigative aid to produce further leads, but the prosecution cannot use that witness's hypnosis interview if it has previously been prohibited.

The witness in the *Chi Omega* case had seen a photograph in the newspaper which Bundy claimed to have influenced her choice from a police array of photographs. The court found in previous cases that an impermissibly suggestive photographic identification did not apply to situations where a witness had earlier observed a picture of a defendant in the news media. Moreover, Bundy claimed the police used a suggestive comment when the officer asked "select the photograph of the person that resembled the suspect." The court did not feel this procedure was impermissibly suggestive.

In the *Eyler* case, there was passenger, Hayward, in Eyler's truck at the initial stop. Instead of treating Hayward as a potential witness or even more obvious, a future victim, Hayward was interviewed as a homosexual co-conspirator. This treatment of Hayward delayed subsequent statements by Hayward that would have given the police probable cause to hold Eyler on separate charges. By the time the police received this statement from Hayward, the court ruled that the illegal seizure of Eyler had already taken place.

In the *Corona* case, Corona's lawyer failed to develop any defenses. The court stated that alibi defenses directly effected the conduct of the police in their interviews of witnesses. The court pointed out that crucial dates and times received from witnesses may have been in conflict and that other people had access to the same evidence and property as did Corona.

Recommendations: Law enforcement officers involved in the investigation of serial killings must be familiar with their particular state's case law regarding the handling of witnesses. The use hypnosis by investigators usually takes place in important high profile cases when other investigative methods have been exhausted. Detectives should carefully weigh the value of the expectations from the hypnosis interview against possibly losing that witness' testimony at a future time. This decision must be coordinated with the prosecuting attorney handling the case. If hypnosis is used, proper voice recordings are necessary to document the interview. This evidence protects the hypnosis session from accusations of suggestibility and influencing the witness. In any statements given by witnesses, detectives must thoroughly document in writing the context of what was said. This protects the credibility of the witness.

Investigators must be cautious in their use of photographic and line-up identification procedures. Case law is filled with many examples of improper liberties taken by the police in using these procedures. Strict guidelines for the use of line-ups and montages should be established with the assistance of the prosecuting attorney.

In the *Bundy* case, the witness saw a newspaper photograph of the suspect prior to viewing the montage of photographs. Because these cases have high news media appeal, the police, in order to demonstrate fairness, must make every effort to assure that the witness is untainted by news accounts. The fact that a witness sees a news photograph before identifying a suspect from photographs or a lineup is legal does not give the right to investigators to suggest to a witness to watch the news first.

In the *Eyler* case, there was no evidence that anyone other than Eyler was a suspect in similar murders. The improper interview of Hayward was just one of a multitude of errors perpetrated by the police. One could almost conclude that one officer's obvious prejudice against homosexuals placed Hayward in a different light and hindered an impartial investigation into the truth of the matter. In a case fraught with legal problems from the beginning, Hayward's interview certainly was indicative of the entire situation. Had Hayward been treated as a victim from the beginning, Eyler's charges may not have been dropped in the series of murder cases.

The rebuttal to a defendant's alibi is very important to the success of a trial. Police must effectively document the statements of all persons interviewed in order to prevent them from changing their story to the benefit of the defendant.

The Initial Confrontation of the Suspect by Police

After Eyler's traffic stop for illegal parking, he was immediately seized for purposes of interrogation regarding certain murders. No probable causes existed for Eyler's detention. He was only named as a possible suspect in the murders. The task force investigating the murders had published a bulletin about Eyler, but the state police officers misinterpreted the bulletin and immediately arrested Eyler for the murders. This improper arrest tainted the search of Eyler's truck and made the seizure of evidence illegal.

In the *Williams* case, Williams claimed that regardless of the legality of the initial interstate stop and any consent he may have subsequently given, his prolonged detention by police exceeded the scope of a *Terry*-type stop and became a full-fledged arrest which was not supported by probable cause. The Supreme Court of Georgia did not agree. It stated that Williams consented to the ensuing detention and search of his car. The consent was given voluntarily and was not the result of duress or coercion. A valid consent eliminated the need for either probable cause to search or a search warrant.

Recommendations: Most police officers are aware of the limitations in questioning and searching a *Terry* stop. In Eyler's case a *Terry*-stop situation did not have a chance to materialize since he was immediately arrested. What police officers might not be familiar with are the permissible ways to obtain the voluntary consent of a suspect to detain, interview or search. The Supreme Court of Illinois expressed the best recommendation to an alternative for the police actions. The officers should have asked Eyler to come to the

police precinct. A voluntary consent to accompany officers to a stationhouse for interrogation had been used by courts to distinguish
permissible stationhouse interrogation on less than probable cause
from arrest due to illegal custodial interrogation.

A major consideration in the investigation of serial murders is
to have a strategy to ask for the voluntary cooperation of a suspect
at the initial confrontation.   This procedure obviated the legal
problems voiced by Williams.   In the *Williams* case, as the court
stated, the critical factor was his own testimony since it established
that he consented to being questioned and having his car searched.
In past serial murder cases, some suspects did cooperate voluntarily
in the beginning of the investigation to the extent that alibi and confession statements were obtained.   Additionally, some limited
searches of the immediate property were accomplished.

A common investigative technique is to publish bulletins for police patrols about the specifics of the ongoing investigation.   The
Eyler case demonstrated how bulletins were misinterpreted at the
expense of the entire case.   Careful thought must go into the con-
tents of bulletins delineating clear and exact procedures to be followed by officers. Policy decisions must be established concerning
the actual utility of the bulletin whether it is "information only" or
"stop and arrest."

The Search of the Suspect's Property

In each of these cases the affidavits for search warrants were
highly scrutinized by the defense attorneys for conflicts, errors,
omissions and inaccurate statements. Gacy attacked the search of
his residence by stating that the affidavit for the search warrant was
defective. He claimed that it failed to disclose sufficient facts to establish probable cause, to state the time when the informants made
their observations and to describe with particularity the items to be
seized. The warrant caused the scope of the search to be too broad.
The court did not sustain Gacy's claims.

A search of Williams's vehicle took place after a legal *Terry*-type
stop and with the voluntary consent of Williams. The court consid-

ered this a valid consent, thus eliminating the need for probable cause to search or a search warrant.

A limited search of Eyler's pickup truck was conducted after he was illegally detained. One state trooper told another that the color of the bag he saw Eyler carrying was not the same one he had initially discovered in Eyler's truck. Another trooper then went to Eyler's truck and discovered some implements of Eyler's murders. The court declared that this search took place without proper authority and incidental to an illegal arrest.

Recommendations: The relevant legal concepts with which investigators must be familiar in order to search a suspect's property are (1) the limitations of a search incidental to a *Terry*-type stop; (2) the requirements of a search incidental to a probable cause arrest; (3) the elements involved in obtaining a valid consent to search; and (4) the probable cause necessary to obtain a valid search warrant. Each of these legal concepts have been attacked on appeal by convicted serial killers.

Summary

Unfortunately, serial murder exists most clearly in the minds of those most likely to engage in it. This certainly should come as no surprise, especially to those law enforcement officers who have been responsible for its investigation. Hampered by traditional approaches to homicide investigation, limited resources and jurisdictional boundaries, coupled with the very nature of the serial killer, police agencies frequently find themselves several steps behind in the investigation.

The single most important aspect of serial murder investigation is the early identification that a serial killer is operating. The five serial murder investigations presented here are evidence that too many victims were murdered before the serial pattern was recognized. What complicates any specific method of recognizing a series is the considerable variation across individual killers in the way in which they approach, murder and dispose of their victims.

Efforts to generalize from the information presented in this book to all serial murder cases must be viewed with caution. Those convicted murderers who have killed two or more and up to twenty victims, and their subsequent appeals, were not the focus of this book. Nor have all those convicted murderers who have killed more than twenty victims been included for this analysis. And, it must be evident that police agencies have also successfully investigated serial murders notwithstanding traditional methods and without forming a multi-agency task force. The logical conclusion, then, is that further research into the factors that determine when it is necessary to form a multi-agency task force needs to be pursued.

Additional research questions could be: What are the specific factors in serial murder recognition? How are serial killers apprehended? What investigative techniques have proven successful in serial murder investigations?

Although there may be a constant gap between what is known about the techniques of serial murder investigation and the actual application of those techniques, police investigators must continually be flexible in their approaches to murder investigation. The investigation of serial murder is difficult under the best of circumstances. The political influences that govern resource expenditures and jurisdictional boundaries further compound the investigation process. This is likely to be the case for quite a while, until police administrators become familiar with the elements involved in serial murder cases. Only then can they convince politicians that unprecedented and extraordinary measures must be taken in planning for and investigating serial murder.

APPENDIX

Comparative Profiles of Homicides Attributed to Wayne Williams

VICTIM:
Jimmy Ray Payne

PROFILE OF VICTIM:
Age: 21
Sex: Male
Race: Black
Height: 5'7"
Weight: 138 lbs.
Home situation:
   Lower income. Victim from broken home, living with mother, sister
   and girlfriend. Recently released from detention center.
Habits:
   Unemployed. No car or driver's license.
   When last seen, victim was on his way to the Omni.

CIRCUMSTANCES OF DEATH:
Date body found: 4/27/81
Place body found: Chattahoochee River, 1/4 mile downstream from
                    I-285 overpass.
Condition of body: Clad only in shorts.
Cause of death: Asphyxiation by undetermined means.

EVIDENCE THAT WILLIAMS MURDERED VICTIM:
Fiber association consistent with Williams's environment: 6. Presence of
animal hairs consistent with hairs from appellant's dog: Yes. Sighting of
Williams in company of victim: Payne disappeared 4-21-81. On 4-22-81
Payne seen with Williams on Highway 78, approximately 1 mile from
Chattahoochee River and near a parked white station wagon. Sighting of
Williams at crime scene or victim's funeral: No.

VICTIM:
Nathaniel Cater

PROFILE OF VICTIM:
Age: 28
Sex: Male
Race: Black
Height: 5'10"
Weight: 146 lbs.
Home situation:
   Lived in downtown Atlanta hotel on Luckie St.
Habits:
   Worked out of labor pool occassionally. Drank a lot. Had no car.
   Frequented downtown lounges, as well as Rialto Theater.

CIRCUMSTANCES OF DEATH:
Date body found: 5-24-81
Place body found: Chattahoochee River, 200 yds. downstream from
                    I-285 overpass.
Condition of body: Nude.
Cause of death: Asphyxiation, probably by chokehold.

EVIDENCE THAT WILLIAMS MURDERED VICTIM:
Fiber association consistent with Williams' environment: 5. Presence of
animal hairs consistent with hairs from appellant's dog: Yes. Sighting od
Williams in company of victim: Two witnesses sighted the victim in the
company of Williams. One saw him during the week before Cater
disappeared. There was a station wagon containing a German Shepherd
dog parked nearby. The other sighting, by the last person to see Cater
alive, was of Williams coming out of the Rialto Theater with victim. The
victim and appellant were holding hands. Sighting of Williams at crime
scene or victim's funeral: Members of a surveillance team stationed on
Jackson Parkway Bridge over the Chattahoochee heard a splash around
3:00 a.m. 5-22-81 and saw a circle of waves form in the river. A white
Chevrolet station wagon driven by Wayne Williams was observed to start
up and cross the bridge and was subsequently stopped by police.

VICTIM:
Alfred Evans

PROFILE OF VICTIM:
Age: 14
Sex: Male
Race: Black
Height: 5'4 1/2"
Weight: 86 lbs.
Home situation:
   Lived in East Lake Meadows Housing Project.
Habits:
   Had no car. Did odd jobs. Was frequently out late.

CIRCUMSTANCES OF DEATH:
Date body found: 7-28-79
Place body found: 11 ft. off Niskey Lake Road, north of Campbellton
                    Rd. in southwest Atlanta. Body dumped down
                    embankment. No sign of atruggle at scene.
Condition of body: Clad in slacks.
Cause of death: Asphyxiation, probably strangulation.

EVIDENCE THAT WILLIAMS MURDERED VICTIM:
Fiber association consistent with Williams' environment: 3. Presence of
animal hairs consistent with hairs from appellant's dog: Yes. Sighting of
Williams in company of victim: No. Sighting of Williams at crime scene
or victim's funeral: No.

VICTIM:
Eric Middlebrooks

PROFILE OF VICTIM:
Age: 14
Sex: Male
Race: Black
Height: 4'10"
Weight: 88 lbs.
Home situation:
   Raised in foster home. Had lived with present foster father since 1965. Older brother officer with Atlanta Police Dept.
Habits:
   Kept fairly late hours. Ran errands for neighbors. Transportation by bicycle.

CIRCUMSTANCES OF DEATH:
Date body found: 5/19/80
Place body found: Off Flat Shoals Rd., less than 1/2 mile from I-20.
Condition of body; Fully clothed.
Cause of death: Blows to the head with blunt ubstrument. Two stab wounds. Body could have been dumped at site.

EVIDENCE THAT WILLIAMS MURDERED VICTIM:
Fiber association consistent with Williams' environment: 4. Presence of animal hairs consistent with hairs from appellant's dog: Yes. Sighting of Williams in company of victim: No. Sighting of Williams at crime scene or victim's funeral: No.

VICTIM:
Charles Stephens

PROFILE OF VICTIM: ·
Age: 12
Sex: Male
Race: Black
Height: 4'9"
Weight: 108 lbs.
Home situation:
   Came from broken home. Lived in public housing project with mother.
Habits:
   Ran errands in neighborhood to make money. Hung around in the streets frequently. Had no car.

CIRCUMSTANCES OF DEATH:
Date body found: 10-10-80, day after he disappeared.
Place body found: 5 miles from home, off Normandary Drive in East Point, Ga.
Condition of body: Laid out next to road, T-shirt, belt, and socks were missing. No sign of struggle at scene.
Cause of death: Asphyxiation, probable suffocation.

EVIDENCE THAT WILLIAMS MURDERED VICTIM:
Fiber association consistent with appellant's environment: 7. Presence of animal hairs consistent with hairs from appellant's dog: Yes. Sighting of Williams in company of victim: No. Sighting of Williams in company of victim: No. Sighting of Williams at crime scene or victim's funeral: No.

VICTIM:
   Terry Pue

PROFILE OF VICTIM:
   Age: 15
   Sex: Male
   Race: Black
   Height: 5'5 1/2"
   Weight: 100 lbs.
   Home situation:
      Pue lived with his mother at a public housing project. Had no car.
      Had attended "challenge school," a home for juveniles.
   Habits:
      Hung out at the Omni and in West End game room.

CIRCUMSTANCES OF DEATH:
   Date body found: 1/23/81
   Place body found: Near I-20 on Sigman Rd. in Rockdale County.
   Condition of body: Fully clothed. Body appeared "laid out."
   Cause of death: Asphyxiation, possible by manual strangulation.

EVIDENCE THAT WILLIAMS MURDERED VICTIM:
   Fiber association consistent with appellant's environment: 4. Presence of
   animal hairs consistent with hairs from appellant's dog: Yes. Sighting of
   Williams in company of victim: A witness saw Pue with Williams about a
   week before the witness learned that his body had been discovered. The
   witness testified that Williams was in a green station wagon. Sighting of
   Williams at crime scene or victim's funeral: Two officers saw Williams at
   the scene where Pue's body was discovered. Williams had camera
   equipment and offered to shoot crime scene photos. Two witnesses saw
   appellant at victim's funeral. Williams was in a white station wagon.

VICTIM:
Lubie Geter

PROFILE OF VICTIM:

Age: 14
Sex: Male
Race: Black
Height: 5'7"
Weight: 103 lbs.
Home situation:
  Lived with parents.
Habits:
  Did odd jobs to make money. Frequented the Omni. Last seen at a
  mall in the Stewart-Lakewood area in Atlanta.

CIRCUMSTANCES OF DEATH:

Date body found: 2/5/81
Place body found: Wooded area 70 ft. off Vandiver Rd., which runs off
                    Campbellton Rd.
Condition of body: Lying on its back with most clothing found nearby.
Cause of death: Asphyxiation, probably strangled with a chokehold.

EVIDENCE THAT WILLIAMS MURDERED VICTIM:

Fiber association consistent with appellant's environment: 4. Presence of
animal hairs consistent with hairs from appellant's dog: Yes. Sighting of
Williams in company of victim: Two witnesses saw Williams with Geter
on the day he disappeared. One originally said Geter was with a man not
wearing glasses. The other testified Geter got into car with man he
identified as Williams. The car was identified as white with black top.
This witness was a fifteen-year-old who testified that he had been
approached by Williams in the same area the previous August and
offered a job. He got into the car with Williams, who fondled him as they
drove around. This witness escaped when Williams stopped and got out
saying he needed something from the trunk. Sighting of Williams at
crime scene or victim's funeral: The juvenile witness testified that
Williams was at the victim's funeral.

VICTIM:
Patrick Baltazar

PROFILE OF VICTIM:
Age: 11
Sex: Male
Race: Black
Height: 5'4 1/2"
Weight: 130 lbs.
Home situation:
From broken home. Lived part time with father in area near Omni.
Habits:
Kept late hours. Did odd jobs to make money. Hung out at the Omni. Frequently on the streets in the area between Foundry St. and the Omni. Had no vehicle.

CIRCUMSTANCES OF DEATH:
Date body found: 2/13/81
Place body found: Corporate Square, an office complex located 3 blocks from I-85.
Condition of body: Fully clothed but clothing unbuttoned.
Cause of death: Probably asphyxiation due to ligature strangulation.

EVIDENCE THAT WILLIAMS MURDERED VICTIM:
Fiber association consistent with appellant's environment: 9. Presence of animal hairs consistent with hairs from appellant's dog: Yes. Sighting of Williams in company of victim: No. Sighting of Williams at crime scene of victim's funeral: No. Additional associations: Two scalp hairs inconsistent with victim's hair but consistent with appellant's hair.

VICTIM:
Larry Rogers

PROFILE OF VICTIM:
Age: 18
Sex: Male
Race: Black
Height: 5'2"
Weight: 130 lbs.
Home situation:
    Lived with foster parents.
Habits:
    Used bike for transportation. Did odd jobs. Played ball with young children at various parks. Rogers was slightly retarded.

CIRCUMSTANCES OF DEATH:
Date body found: 4/9/81
Place body found: Abandonded apartment off Simpson St., less than 1 mile from Bankhead Hgwy.
Condition of body: Clad only in shorts and tennis shoes.
Cause of death: Asphyxiation due to strangulation, possibly by chokehold.

EVIDENCE THAT WILLIAMS MURDERED VICTIM:
Fiber association consistent with appellant's environment: 6. Presence of animal hairs consistent with hairs from appellant's dog: Yes. Sighting of Williams in company of victim: Two friends of the victim placed him with Williams before his disappearance. One saw him three times in one day about three days before he disappeared. Another friend saw him with Williams about the time of his disappearance in a green station wagon. She actually spoke to the victim, who was slumped over and didn't reply. Sighting of Williams at crime scene or victim's funeral: The witness who saw Rogers with Williams on the day he disappeared also saw Williams at the victim's funeral.

VICTIM:
John Porter

PROFILE OF VICTIM:
Age: 28
Sex: Male
Race: Black
Height: 5'10"
Weight: 123 lbs.
Home situation:
   Lives alone in abandoned apartment.
Habits:
   Recently released from Ga. Regional Hospital. Unemployed. Had no vehicle.

CIRCUMSTANCES OF DEATH:
Date body found: 4/12/81
Place body found: Near Capitol Ave. approximately 1 mile from I-20, 3 miles from I-85.
Condition of body: Fully clothed. No evidence of foul play at the scene.
Cause of death: No evidence of drowning. Cause of death set as asphyxiation due to some type of neck manipulation.

EVIDENCE THAT WILLIAMS MURDERED VICTIM:
Fiber association consistent with apppellant's environment: 2. Presence of animal hairs consistent with hairs from appellant's dog: No. Sighting of Williams in company of victim: A friend testified that he had been with Bell when Bell got into a white or sky blue station wagon with appellant the last time Bell was seen alive at the school basketball court. A third witness had gotten a ride with appellant when Bell was in car. Sighting of Williams at crime scene or victim's funeral: No.

VICTIM:
William Barrett

PROFILE OF VICTIM:
Age: 16
Sex: Male
Race: Black
Height: 5'5"
Weight: 130 lbs.
Home situation:
Barrett lived with his mother and was on probation to the Dept. of Human Resources Youth Division. He was last seen by his court services worker prior to his appointment on 5/11/81.
Habits:
Worked odd jobs. Had no car.

CIRCUMSTANCES OF DEATH:
Date body found: 5/12/81
Place body found: Off Winthrop Rd. just off I-20
Condition of body:
Body appeared to have been dumped on the road. Five knife pricks in the body but only two holes in victim's shirt. Clothing was unbuttoned and pants were loose. In addition to knife pricks in the abdomen, there were two horizontal post-mortem stab wounds.
Cause of death: Asphyxia due to strangulation

EVIDENCE THAT WILLIAMS MURDERED VICTIM:
Fiber association consistent with appellant's environment: 6. Presence of animal hairs consistent with hairs from appellant's dog: Yes. Sighting of Williams in company of victim: Barrett's cousin and aunt both testified to Barrett's bringing Williams to their home. Sighting of Williams at crime scene or victim's funeral: No. Additional associations: Blood stains in Williams's 1970 station wagon were consistent with Barrett's blood type A with a blood enzyme type PGM-1, a combination existing in only 24% of the population.[1]

---

[1] *Williams v. State*, at pp. 64-70.

REFERENCES

Brown, Lee P. "Background Material Missing and Murdered Children's Cases." Department of Public Safety, City of Atlanta. 1981.

Bundy v. State, 455 So.2d 330 (Fla. 1984).

Bundy v. State, 471 So.2d 9 (1985).

"Suspect Charged with Killing Teen," *Chicago Tribune*, 23 August 1984, sec. 1, p. 1.

Deadman, Harold A. "Fiber Evidence and the Wayne Williams Trial." *FBI Law Enforcement Bulletin* (May 1984) p. 10.

Gay, L.R. *Educational Research* Columbus, Ohio: Charles E. Merrill Pub. Co., 1976.

Lunde, Donald L. *Murder and Madness*. NY: W.W. Norton Co., 1979.

Nettler, Gwynn. *Killing One Another*. Cincinnati: Anderson Publ. Co., 1982.

People v. Corona, 80 Cal. 3d 684, 145 Cal. Rptr. 894 (1978).

People v. Eyler, 87 Ill. Dec. 648, 132 Ill. App. 3d 792, 477 N.E.2d 774 (1985).

People v. Gacy, 103 Ill. 2d 1, 82 Ill. Dec. 391, 468 N.E.2d 1171 (1984).

Williams v. State, 251 Ga. 749, 312 S.E.2d 40 (Ga. 1983).